A KINGDOM

Deeper into Go

MARK STIBBE

Foreword by Michael Mitton

DARTON · LONGMAN + TODD

First published in Great Britain by
Darton, Longman and Todd Ltd
1 Spencer Court
140–142 Wandsworth High Street
London SW18 4JJ

Copyright © 1994 Mark Stibbe
Illustrations © 1994 Carol Fordham

ISBN 0–232–52064–X

A catalogue record for this book is available from the British Library

Scripture quotations are taken from the New International Version of the Bible
published by Hodder and Stoughton Ltd.

Phototypeset in 11/13pt Ehrhardt by Intype, London
Printed and bound in Great Britain
at the University Press, Cambridge

To Mij (1984–93)

Much loved and sorely missed

CONTENTS

LIST OF ILLUSTRATIONS

ACKNOWLEDGEMENTS

There are a number of people whom I want to thank for their help in preparing this book on prayer.

First and foremost is Carol Fordham, who drew the illustrations of the Temple. These perfectly depict the images which I have in my imagination as I proceed through each of the stages of daily prayer. I am eternally grateful to Carol for her pictures.

Secondly, I want to thank the many people with whom I have shared the vision of this book. The different groups and churches to which I have imparted the material are too numerous to mention, but I do want to thank the people of St Mark's parish, Grenoside, for their encouraging and helpful comments. I shall not forget Lent 1993 for a long time: it was during five evenings together in that season that we, as a church, learnt about our calling as kingdom priests together. There was a profound anointing on those meetings. I learnt a great deal from the people there.

Thirdly, I want to thank my family for the support and love which they have shown. This is now the fifth book I have written in two years. Family life has had to take a back seat during bouts of writing. I am particularly grateful to my wife Alie for her understanding and for her encouragement.

Finally, I want to thank Morag Reeve and her colleagues at Darton, Longman and Todd for their help throughout the process of transforming manuscript into book.

FOREWORD

My first meeting with Mark Stibbe was in the pub opposite St
Thomas's Church in Sheffield during his time as curate there. He
seemed to be known by most of those present who discussed with him
the latest fortunes of Sheffield Wednesday before I was finally able
to have my time with him. Mark is a man who is very much in touch
with the normal things of life, yet at the same time he is someone
who is remarkably gifted as a theologian and someone with a wonderfully attractive spirituality which resources itself from a wide range
of traditions. Here we have a delightful book on prayer which is well
earthed and simply expressed, is theologically competent and imaginative, and has immense potential radically to affect our prayer lives.

There is no doubt in my mind that one of the clearest signals
coming from heaven during our day is a call to prayer. Wherever I
travel in this country or overseas I regularly come across com-
munities of Christian people who are feeling moved to deepen
their prayer life. These are days which are both disturbing and
exciting, as we see the Spirit of God stirring the Church into
deeper spirituality and more effective, compassionate mission.
Mark's book is, therefore, very timely because here is a very practical and biblically based way of deepening our roots in the Vine.

The main message of this book is that we are all priests when it
comes to the work of prayer, and Mark draws upon the principles
of the Jewish Temple to direct us. Regularly we are taken back to
the first century Temple to discover so many fascinating aspects of
its rich and wonderful worship. But we are not left there, because
Mark applies New Testament principles to all of this, and we
discover the wonder of being permitted into the courts of heaven
and drawing near to God. But lest it all remain interesting theory,
he then applies this to our lives today in practical ways, giving us a
five stage, 'user friendly' way into prayer. One of the great things

about this book is that it is so practical, and it also has that crucial dimension of imagination. Carol Fordham's lovely pictures are a great help with this.

This is not a book for those who merely have an academic interest in prayer. It is for those who want to join the adventure of prayer, and there is much in this book that has the potential to change our lives. Some will read it and discover for the first time the awesomeness of God as they gaze upon the throne of heaven; others will discover the intimacy of God as they realize they can actually come in through the gates and be loved. There is much here which has the potential to bring healing to our lives.

I read this book while on retreat on the Isle of Iona one blustery week in January. I have always found structures of prayer difficult, particularly if they involve having to memorise stages. However, because of the imaginative link with the Temple, and because of the illustrations, I found no difficulty in remembering the stages of this prayer journey, and far from being a restrictive structure it brought new freedom to my prayer life.

I used it one afternoon in a long walk across the island, progressing through the gates of thanksgiving calling to mind so many good things God had done for me; moving into the courts of praise and using Mark's wonderful alphabet of the names of Jesus; then kneeling on the western seashore coming in repentance to the altar of sacrifice; from here I walked across the somewhat treacherous marshland and rocks which for me became a holy place as I offered my petitions and intercessions to God very much aware of the spiritual battle; finally I climbed Dun I at the north of the island which became the throne room, and, hardly able to stand in the strong Atlantic gale, I stood looking out over oceans and island to adore our Creator God.

But you do not have to go on pilgrimage to far-off isles to embark on this prayer journey. You can start now wherever you are, at home, at work, or while travelling. This foreword has gone on long enough! Start reading the book. Read with the spirit of an adventurer, for you are in for some great discoveries. May the gentle and powerful Spirit of God fill your sails as you set out.

MICHAEL MITTON
Feast of St Anthony 1994

INTRODUCTION

In 1989 I began to see things in the Scriptures that I had not seen before. Most of these disclosures came from the Old Testament, which until that point I had not read and studied as I should. In particular, I was struck by the first revelation of God to Moses on Mount Sinai, recorded in Exodus 19. Before God gave Moses the Ten Commandments, he uttered one of the most beautiful promises in the entire Bible. He said: 'Although the whole earth is mine, you will be for me a kingdom of priests and a holy nation' (v. 6). The phrase that struck me at the time, and has continued to strike me ever since, was that phrase 'a kingdom of priests'. God wanted the whole people of Israel to be a kingdom of priests! Not just Aaron and the Levites – that group of special people set aside for the office of priesthood – but *everyone* was to be a priest in the kingdom of God.

As I searched the Old Testament even more I began to see that this promise was never fulfilled under the old covenant. When the promise was first given in Exodus 19.6, there was a condition attached. God said, 'If you obey me *fully* . . . you will be for me a kingdom of priests'. The condition was total obedience. Of course, complete personal consecration was not an ongoing reality in the life of the people of Israel. They continually departed from the Lord and did what was wrong in his eyes. In spite of constant reminders and revivals, there never was a consistent and corporate desire to obey God fully, and so disaster followed upon disaster.

But in the midst of all this apostasy, God never forgot that promise which he gave to Moses at Sinai. Even whilst the floods of judgement roared, God never forgot the rainbow of his mercy. From time to time he repeated his promise. Thus in Isaiah 61.6, we find another prophecy, this time a promise of a new era when the Messiah would establish a people who could truly be a kingdom of priests: 'And you will be called priests of the Lord, you will be named ministers of our God'. This promise is part of a long prophecy about the year of the Lord's favour, a prophecy which begins with the famous words, 'The Spirit of the Lord is upon me, because the Lord has anointed me to preach good news to the poor'.

Prophecy Fulfilled

Nearly seven hundred years later, Jesus entered the synagogue in Nazareth, his home town. He opened the scroll for the set reading of the day, which was Isaiah 61 – the Scripture which I have just cited. He read the words of Isaiah 61.1–2, then sat down and said, 'Today this Scripture is fulfilled in your hearing' (Luke 4.16–21).

Isaiah had promised that one day there would be a people called to be priests of the Lord and ministers of God, and that day would be marked by the coming of the Spirit-anointed One of Isaiah 61.1. When Jesus said the words, 'Today this Scripture is fulfilled', he was alerting his audience to a profound and earth-changing reality: the promised day had arrived. Now was the time for God to form a kingdom of priests. Now was the time for God to call people into his royal priesthood. Jesus, the charismatic Messiah foretold by Isaiah, would call those who had ears to hear to a life of Spirit-anointed, priestly ministry. People only had to follow him, and they would become that kingdom of priests of which God had spoken centuries before on Mount Sinai.

Jesus' inaugural sermon at Nazareth is therefore an epochal event. Here the call to the priesthood begins. But it is not until about three years after this that the actual ordination, if you will, takes place. Those three years were, for the disciples, a training for the priesthood. The ordination itself occurred on the day of Pentecost, a day associated in Jewish thought with the giving of the Law to Moses on Mount Sinai. When the day of Pentecost arrived, the Ascended Messiah and Lord literally drenched his disciples with the Holy Spirit, with the consequence that their tongues were released into the priestly ministeries of praise, prophecy and proclamation. From Pentecost onwards, God's kingdom of priests was and is firmly established. All we have to do is to hear and obey the call.

2

The Temple of Prayer

At the time of noticing this call to the priesthood, I was beginning to experience a crisis in my prayer life. Up until 1989, I had been using a model of prayer which was given to me after my conversion in 1977. This was the A-C-T-S model:

A – doration, or praising God
C – onfession, or repenting of sin
T – hanksgiving
S – upplication, or praying for myself and for others.

This had served me well for a long time, but it was now beginning to feel restrictive. Somehow it seemed to lack the colour, the depth and the variety which true prayer is all about. Prayer is, after all, like love; it is a many-splendoured thing. It is a gem capable of many different refractions. Yet for me it had become a mono-chrome ritual: adoration, followed by confession, followed by thanksgiving, followed by supplication. There was little true devotion, no listening or contemplation, a lot of emphasis upon myself, and a great deal of repetition.

At the same time as this, I also started an intensive study of priesthood in ancient Israel. The more I became convinced that God wanted me to be a priest of his kingdom, the more I became fascinated by the priestly ministeries of the Old Testament, because in those I felt there might be a type of what we, in the new covenant, might be called to do today. I very quickly noticed how central the Temple in Jerusalem was to the Levites or priests. In 1 Chronicles 23 we read:

> The duty of the Levites was to help Aaron's descendants in the service of the temple of the Lord: to be in charge of the courtyards, the side rooms, the purification of all sacred things and the performance of other duties at the house of God (v. 28).

As I began to appreciate the importance of the Temple, I also began to see that the Temple ministries of the Levitical priests could fruitfully be used as a model of what we could do in prayer today. Subsequently, I started to use the priest's daily duties in the

3

Temple as the basis for a new and richer prayer life – one in which I began to live out my priesthood.

The Temple Ministries

Further research revealed that there had been three Temples in Jerusalem. The first one was constructed by King Solomon in the middle of the tenth century BC (1 Kings 5–8; 2 Chronicles 3–4) and was destroyed by the Babylonians in 585 BC. The second Temple was built by those who returned from Babylonian exile (Ezra 3.8–13) and was dedicated in 515 BC (Ezra 6.16–18). The third Temple was an enlargement and restoration of this structure, supervised by Herod the Great in 20 BC.

The plan of the Temple followed the design of the Tabernacle, and probably looked like this:

THE TEMPLE

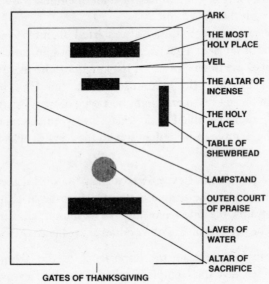

GATES OF THANKSGIVING

The priest on duty would enter through the gates of thanks-giving. At the heart of the court of praise was the altar of sacrifice where he would offer blood sacrifices for the forgiveness of sins. Past that was the laver of water, a great bronze basin where the priest would wash before entering the holy place. This was illuminated by golden lampstands, known as the *menorah*, which had seven golden candlesticks. On the right-hand side of the holy place were the golden tables of shewbread where the priest presented and consecrated pieces of bread. At the heart of the holy place was the golden altar where the priest burnt incense in the morning and the evening. This incense represented the prayers of God's people ascending into heaven. Finally, beyond the veil, was the cherubim throne in the most holy place. Only the high priest, once every year, was allowed to enter this innermost sanctuary.

The Temple as a Model of Prayer

As soon as I saw this plan of the Temple, I became excited. I felt straight away that God was providing a creative structure for prayer. Confirmation of this came almost immediately when I remembered how the Bible actually associates the Temple with prayer. Did Isaiah not prophesy a time when the Temple would be called '*a house of prayer* for all nations' (Isaiah 56.7)? Does Jesus himself not call the Temple in Jerusalem '*a house of prayer*' (Matthew 23.13)?

It seemed to me, then, that the design of the Temple could be used as the basis for ministering to God and I put it into practice in my own prayer life. I begin by entering the gates of God's presence with thanksgiving. I then spend time in the court of praise, worshipping God for who he is. I pause at the new altar of sacrifice, the Cross of Jesus, in order to put my sins to death. I then wash at the laver of water before ascending the steps to the great entrance to the holy place. After this I spend time at the table of shewbread and the golden lampstands, petitioning for my daily physical and spiritual needs. I then proceed to the golden altar of incense, to offer intercessions to God. Finally, I pass through the torn veil to enter the most holy place, where it was believed one could see the throne of God. Here I spend time in devotional prayer.

All this can be reduced to five stages of prayer which imitate the ministries of the priests in the Temple. In the simplest form they look like this:

THE FIVE STAGES OF PRAYER

1. **The Gates of Thanksgiving = Thanking God**

2. **The Court of Praise = Praising God**

3. **The Altar of Sacrifice = Repentance**

4. **The Altar of Incense = Intercession**

5. **The Most Holy Place = Beholding the Throne**

The Virtues of this Model

As I have used this model, I have found a number of virtues in this approach to personal prayer. Other people who now use this discipline have confirmed the fact that:

6

INTRODUCTION

It is easy to remember

There is something about using the plan of a house, or any kind of building, which appeals to the faculty of human memory. Somehow, using rooms and furniture as mnemonics is a very effective way of structuring what one wants to say. Thus ancient orators like Cicero, when they gave a speech in politics or in the lawcourts, used to remember everything they had prepared to say by using the model of a Roman house. The hall would be their introduction, and various items of decor in the hall would be used to represent various features of this introduction. So the process would go on: the speech would end once the speaker's mind had roamed through all the rooms in his imagined house of memory.

One of the reasons why people have found the Temple model helpful is because, like the Roman villa, it provides a basic structure for what one wants to say, and at the same time contains obvious mnemonics or memory aids. The gates of thanksgiving, for example, are where we pray prayers of thanksgiving; the altar of sacrifice is where we put sin to death, and so on. All the aspects of the Temple function as reminders of what we have to do as we minister to God in prayer.

It occupies the imagination

But this way of praying not only appeals to the memory. It also appeals to the imagination. We all of us struggle to keep our imaginations under control when we pray. Hardly a moment passes before the imagination is up to its old tricks again, putting images and fantasies of the most distracting nature into our minds. Perhaps this is why Simone Weil wrote, in her book *Gravity and Grace*, that 'the imagination is constantly at work filling in the fissures through which grace would pass'.

However, focusing on a building as we go through stages of prayer is a very effective way of giving the imagination something else to think about! Many of the saints have discovered this to be true. I think in particular of Teresa of Avila who confessed to feeling 'exasperated' by the antics of her imagination in prayer. She described her imagination as 'restless, confused, and excited, and apparently not centred on God at all, in a word distracted'.[1]

7

To combat this, Teresa came up with the idea of an 'interior castle' as a structure for daily prayer. Basing this model somewhat loosely on John 14, she constructed a castle of seven 'mansions'. These mansions represented different forms of prayer, the first beginning with preparatory disciplines, the last with prayer designed for the highest forms of union between us and the Father. So Teresa begins her classic work on prayer with the words,

> The soul seems to me
>   to be like a castle,
> made of a single diamond
> or of very clear crystal
> in which there are many rooms,
> just as in heaven
> there are many mansions.[2]

Many others have found that using the image of a building or a house is of great benefit for undistracted prayer. Catherine of Sienna, for example, used to think of her soul as an inner cell of prayer. More recently, Andrew Murray used to speak of entering the inner chamber of the heart. These great men and women of prayer have used architectural symbolism in their prayer life as a means of directing the imagination away from the flesh. The Temple model of prayer is helpful for the same reasons.

It involves a gradual approach to God

A third virtue of the Temple model is that it is gradual. What do I mean by gradual? Today we live in an instant culture. We can tune into just about anything just by pressing a button. This has inevitably affected us as Christians. We do tend to tune into God straight away, to hurry into the holy of holies without any pause in our talk, any reverence in our step. There is a positive side to this in that it reveals confidence in our approach to the throne. It shows that we are certain of God's acceptance, sure of his welcome. However, there is a negative side too. It reveals a degree of over-familiarity and presumption. Instead of proceeding towards the innermost sanctuary with a holy fear, we rush in where angels fear to tread.

In the Temple in Jerusalem, however, everything was designed to create a gradual and respectful approach to God. First of all, there was a division of the outer and inner areas of the Temple. In New Testament Greek this distinction is suggested by the two words which we translate as 'Temple'. The first is *hieron* which denotes the outer court or precincts of the Temple. The second is *naos*, which indicates the inner area – the sanctuary building where the holy place and the holy of holies were situated. The high priest entering the holy of holies on the Day of Atonement would have to go through the *hieron*, the outer court, and then proceed into the *naos*, the sanctuary building. A gradual approach to God is suggested by the use of these two different words for Temple.

It is secondly suggested by the use of two different metals. In the outer court, most of the Temple furniture was fashioned out of bronze. The altar of sacrifice was made of bronze; the laver of water was also made of bronze. Once we enter the sanctuary building, the *naos*, everything changes. The candlesticks are made of gold. The table of shewbread is made of gold. The altar of incense is made of gold. Everywhere you look there is gold. To a Jewish mind this can only mean one thing: the nearer you get to the holy of holies, the more precious, sacred and awesome is the experience.

The Temple model of prayer is therefore ideally suited for a gradual approach to God.

The Call to Priesthood

So the design of the Temple has proved invaluable in developing a priestly model of prayer. Indeed, this book is a distillation of what I have learnt as I have sought to minister in the new spiritual Temple which God is building on earth. As St John saw, when he was caught up in the Spirit on the Island of Patmos, God has made us 'a kingdom *and* priests to serve our God' (Revelation 1.6). This is our destiny, this is our great vocation in the Lord Jesus Christ; to be both God's kingdom *and* God's priests.

One reason why I have written this book is because in recent years we have heard a lot about the first part of that statement (the kingdom), but we have not heard so much about the second part (the priesthood). We have heard a lot about preaching the kingdom, healing the sick and delivering the demonized. We have heard less about ministering to God as priests in the holy Temple of his presence.

My prayer is that by the end of our journey through this book, we will have made a decision to live out our priesthood, and to say with King David,

> One thing I ask of the Lord,
> this is what I seek:
> that I may dwell in the house of the Lord
> all the days of my life,
> to gaze upon the beauty of the Lord
> and to seek him in his temple (Psalm 27.4).

PRAYER

Lord God, I thank you that you have called me to the royal priesthood. I thank you that my greatest priority is to minister to you in the Temple of your holy presence. As I come to prayer now, I ask you to increase the anointing for priesthood upon my life. I ask you to help me through the stages of prayer – the gates of thanksgiving, the courts of praise, the altar of incense, the holy place, the innermost sanctuary. Lead me by your Spirit into the very heart of your holy presence. I pray this in the name of Jesus, our Great High Priest. Amen.

1
THE GATES OF THANKSGIVING

*'The first rule of true prayer is to have heart and mind
in the right mood for talking with God.'*

John Calvin, *Institutes*

The initial stage of prayer is always critical. Many people find that the hardest thing of all is actually beginning. In that respect, prayer can be a little like physical exercise. It is fine once you get started, often enjoyable; but the motivation to do it in the first place is often a matter of sheer discipline, a matter of stubborn will-power. In our prayer life we will discover that this initial obstacle is overcome through proper preparation. Physical exercise requires good preparation – psyching yourself up mentally, warming up physically. So does the daily spiritual exercise of prayer.

The Invocation of the Holy Spirit

The most important act of 'warming up' is to ask the Holy Spirit to empower us for our ministry as priests of the kingdom. This is vital because we are all pulled away from prayer by three different and very powerful forces: the world, the flesh and the devil.

The world pulls us away because it constantly sets before us a whole variety of distractions. Some of these are the distractions of noise. John Donne knew this only too well. He once said, 'I throw myself down in my room, and I invite God and His angels thither; and when they come there, I neglect God for the noise of a fly, the rattle of a coach and the whining of a door'.[1] Other distractions come in the form of ambitious dreams or daily tasks which clamour for our attention. The world says, 'You haven't got time to pray today. There's too much to do in the home, at the office, wherever'.

The flesh pulls us away from prayer because, as Richard Lovelace puts it, 'our fallen nature is actually allergic to God'.[2] The constant inclination of our flesh is towards self-sufficiency. Our spirits, when joined to God's Holy Spirit, incline in the opposite direction. They tell us that self-sufficiency is sin, that we are called to be dependent upon an all-sufficient God. The basic instinct of the flesh is therefore hostile to prayer.

If the world and the flesh pull us away from prayer, so does the devil. As Richard Lovelace goes on to say, 'there is a force in our minds resisting prayer like a solid barrier'. This force belongs to the devil, the enemy of our souls. He is 'painfully aware of the destructive force of even our dullest and weakest prayers and will go to any length to block them'.[3]

With the world, the flesh and the devil obstructing our path to prayer, the odds are stacked against us right from the start. This shows how important it is to ask God's Holy Spirit to silence the clamouring and insistent voices of these three enemies of prayer. Thus Andrew Murray is right to say: 'The great lesson for every prayer is – see to it, first of all, that you commit yourself to the leading of the Holy Spirit, and with entire dependence on Him, give Him the first place; for through Him your prayer will have a value you cannot imagine, and through Him also you will learn to speak out your desires in the name of Christ'.[4]

As we begin our daily ministrations in the Temple of prayer, we therefore need to recognize what we are up against, and we need to petition for the empowering of the Spirit. We must begin with what the Orthodox Church calls the *epiklesis*, the invocation of the Holy Spirit. As we do so, we will find that discipline turns into desire. We will find ourselves saying, with the psalmist:

> Blessed are those who dwell in your house;
>   they are ever praising you.
> Better is one day in your courts
>   than a thousand elsewhere;
> I would rather be a doorkeeper in the
>   house of my God
>   than dwell in the tents of the wicked (Psalm 84.4,10).

Spontaneity within a Structure

We begin our prayers with the *epiklesis* in order to override the destructive inclinations of the world, the flesh and the devil. We also invoke the Holy Spirit so that we can enjoy supernatural spontaneity in our prayers. This is important because the Temple model of prayer is overtly structural in character. We begin with the gates of thanksgiving, we then enter the court of praise, we pause at the altar of sacrifice, wash at the laver of water, enter the holy place, make petitions at the table of shewbread and the golden

13

lampstands, intercede at the altar of incense, before entering the holy of holies in an attitude of devotional prayer. All this involves a framework, a plan, a structure.

Structure is, of course, helpful, especially when one is exhausted and weak. As T.S. Eliot said of poetry, 'Organization is necessary as well as inspiration'.[5] What is true of poetry is also true of prayer. In prayer we do need some kind of mental superstructure to provide the outline and direction for what we do. However, the reverse of what T.S. Eliot said is also true: 'Inspiration is necessary as well as organization'. Relying too much on structure is an obstacle to what the rabbis called *hitlahavaut* – fervour in prayer.[6] Structure can actually quench the Spirit from revealing the mind of Christ to us. That is why we must begin with an *epiklesis*. We need the Holy Spirit to bring reality and power (*hitlahavaut*) to our prayers. Without the touch of God's Spirit, our prayer will be all form and no fire.

The Zechariah Experience

There is a story in Scripture which illustrates this well. It can be regarded as a parable of our need to be open to the unexpected, the supernatural, the exceptional in our priestly ministry of prayer.

Luke 1 records some experiences of John the Baptist's father, Zechariah. According to Luke, Zechariah was a priest. He was a very godly man who observed all the Lord's commandments and regulations. One day, Zechariah was chosen to be the one who went into the Temple to burn incense at the golden altar in the holy place. Zechariah went in to perform his priestly duty, while everyone else waited outside in the court of praise, worshipping God.

All, at first, went smoothly. Zechariah went to the table of shewbread and placed new loaves upon them. He went to the golden candlesticks, put new candles in and lit them. He then went to the golden altar, placed new incense on the censers and lit that. As the smoke ascended to the roof of the Temple, Zechariah started his priestly liturgy, his hands raised towards heaven. At that moment, Luke says – in a somewhat matter of fact way, as if it were a common occurrence – 'an angel appeared to Zechariah'. This angel materialized at the right-hand side of the altar where Zechariah was praying. Zechariah, says Luke, was 'startled', which, of course, is an understatement. However, the angel reassures Zechariah, and tells him some good and unexpected news about becoming a father – a message which probably startled Zechariah more than the messenger.

Zechariah shows a distinct lack of faith at this point – not surprisingly, since in his eyes he has passed the age of fathering children – and he subsequently earns a rebuke from the angel, who reveals that he is Gabriel. The rebuke involves a punishment: Zechariah will not be able to speak again until the child is born.

And so Zechariah comes out of the Temple to find the crowds waiting, wondering why it is that he has spent so long doing what was a routine, liturgical duty. They will be none the wiser for a while, because Zechariah's lips have been supernaturally sealed. So Zechariah returns home to his wife Elizabeth and finds his voice again only when his baby, John the Baptist, is born.

Gift brings sadness

Open to the Supernatural

This colourful tale cautions us against regarding our daily ministry to God as a routine task. Ministering to God in the Temple of prayer is the very opposite of that. We too may be surprised by God. We too may experience a strong anointing or burden from the Holy Spirit. We too may receive a prophetic word for the Church. We may even come face to face with an angel.

And so the opening *epiklesis*, the opening invocation of the Holy Spirit, is a vital ingredient in our prayer time. It makes room for God to move in whatever way he sovereignly chooses. It makes room for the Zechariah experience.

The Gates of Thanksgiving

Once we have prepared ourselves in this way, we are ready to enter the gates of thanksgiving, one of three thresholds we will cross as we proceed through the Temple of prayer. The first threshold is

15

the entrance to the court of praise; the second is the entrance to the holy place; the third is the entrance to the holy of holies.

As we pause at the gates of thanksgiving, it is helpful to remember the exhortation in Psalm 100.4: 'Enter his gates with thanksgiving and his courts with praise; give thanks to him and praise his name'. Here the psalmist is using the design of the Temple as a model for approaching God in worship. He knows that the first two stages of the journey into the sanctuary are the entrance to the inner court of the priests, which he describes as 'the gates of thanksgiving', and the courts themselves, which he calls 'the courts of praise'.

While this is probably an example of Hebrew parallelism – saying the same thing in two slightly different ways – many people find it helpful to distinguish between thanksgiving and praise. Although it may be a slightly artificial division (in terms of the psalmist's understanding), many argue that thanksgiving has to do with God's acts; praise has to do with God's being. In thanksgiving, we thank God for what he has done. In praise, we worship God for who he is.

In thanking God we therefore focus on God's deeds – the revelation of his Name, the Exodus, the giving of the Law, the promise of the Messiah, the Incarnation, the Cross, the Resurrection, the giving of the Spirit. In praising God we focus on God's character and nature – his beauty, his majesty, his mercy, his holiness, his power, his otherness, his love, his compassion, his bounty, his faithfulness, his greatness and his truth.

Thanksgiving in the Old Testament

In many places the Bible stresses the importance of thanksgiving. The Old Testament is full of heartfelt expressions of gratitude to God. The Book of Psalms is a particularly rich reservoir of gratitude:

> *Psalm 7.17* 'I will give thanks to the Lord because of his righteousness . . .'

16

Psalm 28.7 'My heart leaps for joy and I will give thanks to him in song . . .'

Psalm 35.18 'I will give you thanks in the great assembly . . .'

Psalm 75.1 'We give thanks to you, O God, we give thanks for your Name is near . . .'

Psalm 107.1 'Give thanks to the Lord for he is good . . .'

Psalm 118.28 'You are my God, and I will give you thanks . . .'

Clearly thanksgiving was an essential part of prayer for King David (who wrote many of the psalms).

What is true for David is true for his son Solomon. Solomon, like David, often burst enthusiastically into thanksgiving known as a *berakah*, a prayer which begins with the words 'Blessed be God': 'Blessed be the Lord, the God of Israel, who with his own hand has fulfilled what he promised with his own mouth to my father David' (1 Kings 8.15). The same dedication ends with a *berakah* of thankfulness: 'Blessed be the Lord, who has given rest to his people Israel just as he promised' (1 Kings 8.56).

This use of the *berakah*, it should be noted, is found in the psalms as well. Indeed, each of the books of the Psalter concludes with a *berakah* to the Lord (Psalms 41.13; 72.18,19; 89.52; 106.48).

Thanksgiving in Judaism

This Old Testament emphasis on gratitude left its mark on Jewish prayer. The most important formula of prayer in the Jewish liturgy became the *berakah*. This word literally means 'blessing' and is always a prayer of thanks.

Here are a few examples: before drinking a glass of wine, a Jew will say, 'Blessed art thou, O Lord our God, King of the Universe, who createst the fruit of the vine'. Before eating bread, a Jew will exclaim, 'Blessed art thou, O Lord our God, King of the Universe, who bringest forth bread from the earth'. Before reading the Torah, a Jew will pray, 'Blessed art thou, O Lord our God, King of the Universe, who hast given us the Law of truth, and hast planted everlasting life in our midst. Blessed art thou, O Lord, Giver of the Torah'.

Blessing God for his gifts is therefore a characteristic of Jewish prayer. Indeed, one of the eighteen benedictions recited regularly in the Jewish synagogues is a fine example of this desire to thank the Lord for his gracious blessings:

> We give thanks unto thee, for thou art the Lord our God and the God of our fathers for ever and ever; thou art the Rock of our lives, the Shield of our salvation through every generation. We will give thanks unto thee and declare thy praise for our lives which are committed unto thy hand and for our souls which are in thy charge, and for thy miracles which are daily with us, and for thy wonders and thy benefits, which are wrought at all times, evening, morn and noon. O thou who art all good, whose mercies fail not; thou merciful Being, whose loving kindnesses never cease, we have ever hoped in thee. Blessed art thou, O Lord, whose Name is all-good, and unto whom it is becoming to give thanks.[7]

Thanksgiving in the Life of Jesus

As we turn to the gospels, we find a similar importance attached to thanksgiving. This should not surprise us; Jesus himself was a Jew, and he would have heard many a *berakah* during his life. He would also have known those many commands to thank God, whose presence we have noted in the Hebrew Bible.

Jesus' prayers to his Father are sometimes expressed in the form of a *berakah*. One famous example is in Matthew 11.25 (Luke 10.21), when Jesus thanks God for the spiritual insights which Peter has just shown: 'I thank thee, Father, Lord of heaven and earth, that thou hast hidden these things from the wise and understanding and revealed them to babes'. In all probability, this prayer originally began with the formula, 'Blessed art thou'.

Likewise, when Jesus gave thanks for the bread with which he fed the five thousand, he almost certainly would have used a *berakah* (Mark 6.41). Other examples can be found in the narratives concerning the institution of the eucharist (Mark 14.22–4 and parallels). At the Last Supper, Jesus would have recited a *berakah* after he had taken the bread (or the wine). In our versions we simply read 'he blessed it' but in reality this would have been a prayer of thanksgiving, beginning 'Blessed art thou, O Lord our God . . .'

The One Grateful Leper

If Jesus practised thanksgiving, he also preached it. We know this from a short story told only in Luke's gospel (17.11–19). There Luke describes an incident which occurred *en route* to Jerusalem.

Jesus is seen travelling on the border between Samaria and Galilee. He is about to enter a village when ten men with leprosy shout out, 'Jesus, Master, have pity on us!' They are on the out-skirts of the village because lepers were not allowed any nearer to habitation than that. Jesus does indeed have pity on them. He tells them to go and show themselves to the priests. If someone was a leper, he only showed himself to a priest if he had been healed of leprosy. So the fact that the ten immediately go and do so shows not only that they are obedient (because they go); it shows that they are full of faith (because they believe without any tangible evidence).

As they leave for their local priests, the story rather tersely remarks that 'they were cleansed'. That means that they were healed as they walked. Nine of them carry on their journey. One decides to come running back to Jesus. He throws himself at Jesus' feet and thanks him. That man, says Luke, was not a Jew he was a Samaritan.

At this point, Jesus speaks out. He says, 'Where are the other nine of you? There were ten healed. Are you the only to come back and say thank you? Where are the thankless nine?'

Clearly Jesus not only practised thanksgiving, he also preached it. His words in Luke's story show how vital it is for Christians not only to be a people of obedience (who 'go' when Jesus says 'go') and a people of faith (who 'believe' without seeing) but also a people of gratitude (who come back to Jesus to say 'thank you').

Thanksgiving in the New Testament

But thanksgiving is not confined to Jesus alone in the New Testament. When we move on from the gospels, we find that thanksgiving figures prominently in the writings of Paul. The New Testament word for *berakah* is *eucharistia*, from which we get 'eucharist'. *Eucharistia* means thanksgiving, a word found often in the letters of Paul. For example, Paul uses the Greek verb *eucharasteo* when he speaks of the necessity of gratitude in the lifestyle of the Christian disciple. Christians are to have a 'gratitude attitude'. As Paul puts it in Colossians 3.17: 'Whatever you do, whether in word or deed, do it all in the name of the Lord Jesus, *giving thanks* (*eucharisteo*) to God the Father through him'. Earlier in this letter, Paul urges his readers to be 'overflowing with thankfulness' (*eucharistia*, Colossians 2.7), to revel in the use of *berakah*.

Paul stresses that this grateful heart is particularly important in the discipline of prayer. He exhorts the Colossian church members to 'devote yourselves to prayer, being watchful *and thankful*' (*eucharistia*, 4.2). In Philippians 4.6, he says, 'Do not be anxious about anything, but in everything, by prayer and petition, with thanksgiving (*eucharistia*), present your requests to God'.

Thanksgiving is therefore vital to prayer. According to the overall teaching of the New Testament, we are all priests, and we are all called to exercise a eucharistic ministry, to begin our prayers with the ministry of thanksgiving. As Andrew Murray puts it: 'Thanksgiving will draw our hearts out to God and keep us engaged with Him; it will take our attention from ourselves and give the Spirit room in our hearts'.[8] Thanksgiving, one might say, is the 'open sesame' into God's holy presence.

Gratitude and Grace

Most of us recognize the truth of all this. We know that gratitude is important in theory. In practice, however, we often find it hard to muster up a sincere and heartfelt expression of gratitude. We find it difficult to know where to begin.

If we look again at the word *eucharistia*, or thanksgiving, we shall discover that there is a way through this. Tucked away in the centre of *eucharistia* is the beautiful word, *charis*, which means grace. Grace, one might say, is at the heart of gratitude. *Charis* is at the centre of *eucharistia*. This highlights the fact that our level of gratitude will exist in proportion to our awareness of God's grace. The more we are conscious of God's grace, the more grateful we will be. The less conscious we are of his grace, the less it will be natural for us to thank him with joy.

It is helpful, then, to meditate on God's unmerited love for us before we start trying to thank him. Once we remember that God has loved us to death on the Cross, and that this love is totally free and undeserved, we will find it hard to be guilty of ingratitude. Once we catch sight of the amazing grace of God, crying out from the tortured face of Jesus, we can never be ungrateful.

To be a truly eucharistic priesthood we therefore need to reinstate God's costly grace at the centre of our theology. It is sinful to be ungrateful in the presence of such a gracious Father. As King Lear exclaims, 'How sharper than a serpent's tooth it is to have a thankless child'. If we are not to wound our Heavenly Father with the sharp sting of ingratitude, we must constantly remind ourselves of his grace.

The Fullness of God's Grace

As I pass through the gates of thanksgiving, I find it useful to base my prayers of gratitude on the words of John 1.16: 'Out of the fullness of God's grace, we have all received one blessing after another'. This is a magnificent reminder of the extravagant grace of God. God is not miserly. He does not hold to a single or a second blessing theology. Our God believes in giving us continual blessings: 'one blessing after another'.

What, then, are those many blessings for which we can give thanks to God? Here it is important to develop a holistic view of grace. In other words, it is important to develop a worldview in which we are able to discern traces of God's grace in every part of our lives, not just in the spiritual things. We need to learn to give thanks for the blessings we have received in the physical, the emotional, the intellectual, the material, the relational as well as the spiritual dimensions of life. Nothing is too small, too insignificant, too profane, too worldly. The Father loves to be thanked for everything!

In this matter we have much to learn from the Jews. Unlike modern, Western Christians, the Jewish people have never restricted God's blessings to the spiritual sphere of life. They have set prayers of thanksgiving for almost everything because they see the whole universe as a sanctuary of God's benediction. There is no place, no time, no activity, which is immune from thanksgiving. Consequently, Berakhot 54a, in the Mishnah, reminds the Jewish people that:

> One who sees a place where miracles have been worked on behalf of Israel should say: 'Blessed is he who worked miracles for our fathers in this place.' One who sees a place in which a foreign worship was rooted out should say: 'Blessed is he who rooted foreign worship out of our land.' Of comets, storms, thunder, wind and lightning, one should say: 'Blessed is he whose strength and power fill the world.' Of mountains, hills, rivers and deserts one should say: 'Blessed is he who accomplishes the work of creation.'[9]

In relation to gratitude, the Jewish people are therefore much closer to New Testament Christianity than those of us who call ourselves Christians. For 1 Timothy 4.3 says, 'Everything God created is good, and nothing is to be rejected if it is received with thanksgiving (*eucharistia*), because it is consecrated by the word of God and prayer'.

Counting Our Blessings

Consequently, our first ministry after the *epiklesis*, the prayer 'Come, Holy Spirit', is the ministry of thanksgiving. In this ministry we look at every aspect of our lives since we last prayed, and if we did not thank God at the time, we thank him now. We literally count all our blessings. We exclude nothing. We bless the God who blesses us.

22

There are, generally speaking, six kinds of blessing which – in my experience – encourage and evoke our thanksgiving. In each of these cases, it is a wholesome thing to offer up a *berakah* each day. A simple prayer beginning 'I bless you, dear Father, for blessing me with . . .' is all that may be required.

Spiritual blessings

It is important not to neglect our spiritual blessings. In particular, it is essential to remember to thank God that we have a relationship with him at all. It should never cease to excite us that we can pray with the Lord of heaven and earth because he pursued us into a personal relationship with him. It should be a constant source of gratitude that God has, because of his grace, established a relationship of intimacy with us. This is the best of all God's blessings.

The poet, Coleridge, expressed this thought very powerfully a few days before he died:

> I have known what the enjoyments and advantages of this life are, and what the more refined pleasures which learning and intellectual power can bestow; and with all the experience that more than threescore years can give, I now, on the eve of my departure, declare to you . . . that health is a great blessing, competence obtained by honourable industry a great blessing, and a great blessing it is to have kind, faithful, and loving friends and relatives; but that the greatest of all blessings, as it is the most enabling of all privileges, is to be indeed a Christian.[10]

An example from Ephesians

One of the finest *berakhot* or prayers of thanksgiving can be found in Ephesians 1.3–14. This passage is a prayer of gratitude for the spiritual blessings which we have received in Christ. These twelve verses form a single sentence in Greek; indeed, it is twenty-six lines long in the United Bible Societies' text. Clearly, Paul was so effusive in his gratitude to God that he lost his usual control of grammar: Ephesians 1.3–14 is a torrent of thankfulness!

Paul begins his *berakah* with the words, 'Blessed be the God and Father of our Lord Jesus Christ, who has blessed us in the heavenly realms with every spiritual blessing in Christ'. Here the thanksgiving is focused on the blessings received from God the Father. In the next nine verses, the thanksgiving is focused on the blessings received through God the Son (vv. 4–13a). Paul literally overflows with his grounds for gratitude:

> 'he chose us in him before the creation of the world . . .'
> 'in love he predestined us . . .'
> 'in him we have redemption . . .'
> 'he made known to us the mystery of his pleasure . . .'
> 'in him we were also chosen . . .'
> 'and you were also included!'

In the third part of the *berakah*, Paul's thanksgiving is focused upon the blessings received through God the Spirit (vv. 13b–14): 'you were marked in him with a seal, the promised Holy Spirit . . .'

Paul's prayer is a fine example of how to count one's spiritual blessings. It is thoroughly Trinitarian; it rejoices in the blessings from the Father, blessings from the Son, blessings from the Holy Spirit. It is magnificently broad in sweep, going right back to the beginning of creation, and extending forward to the very end of the world, when the times will have reached their fulfilment (v. 10). It is, as I have already mentioned, made up of one single and passionate sentence. There can surely be few finer examples of thanksgiving in the whole of Christian literature.

The centre of gratitude and the grace of adoption

At the centre of Paul's prayer of gratitude is grace. At the mid-point of the passage, Paul speaks about the 'riches of God's grace that he *lavished* on us with all wisdom and understanding'. Paul particularly grateful for God's grace because 'In love he pre-destined us to be adopted as his sons through Christ Jesus' (v. 5). For Paul, the reality of adoption forms the centre of his gratitude.

If that was true for Paul, it has also been true for me. Nothing puts me in touch with the true depths of God's grace more quickly than remembering that I am an adopted child of God. I relate to this metaphor of adoption because I am, in human terms, an adopted child. My twin sister and I were orphaned at birth and adopted by my present parents, Philip and Joy. Claire and I know nothing at all of our natural family. The bonding with Philip and Joy has not been painless but it is strong. Today they and I are closer than many who have been together from conception!

At the very centre of my soul there is therefore a very strong appreciation of the fact that I was an orphan, that I could have remained an orphan, and that my life could have gone in many far less privileged directions. This has profoundly influenced my ability to thank God for his grace. Paul speaks in Ephesians 1.5 of a God who predestined us to be adopted as his sons and daughters. Through the love and the grace of God, we are made the brothers and sisters of Jesus and the children of God. We are given a new, Christ-centred family.

If you have been happily adopted yourself, this kind of theology strikes some deep chords. You suddenly begin to see things very clearly: God is the perfect Father who looked out across the world he had made and saw his children as spiritual orphans. He saw them wandering aimlessly in sin, suffering from what Peter Berger calls 'a sense of homelessness in the cosmos'. What was he to do?

What he did was he asked his Son Jesus to come into the orphanage of our world in order to adopt us into his family. When Jesus said to his disciples, 'I will not leave you orphans' (John 14.18), he was expressing the very heart of God. He was revealing a Father who cannot bear to see his children suffer the agony of spiritual homelessness. He was revealing a God who longs for restored relationship with humanity.

Being an adopted child has therefore helped me to count my spiritual blessings! I am deeply grateful that my Heavenly Father established an eternal relationship with me, that he adopted me through the saving work of Jesus, and that he gave me his Spirit, the Spirit who enables me to cry out to God, 'Abba! Dear Father!' (Galatians 4.6). It always feels like the most natural thing to thank God for the gift of relationship with him. It is as natural as being grateful to my adoptive parents for their initiative of love.

Physical blessings

Of all the blessings which we receive, it is probably the ones relating to our spirituality which we most quickly remember. But if these are the only ones which fuel the flames of our thanksgiving then the chances are we have become a little too spiritual. God's blessings, after all, shower the whole of our lives.

One of the blessings which should promote thanksgiving is the gift of good health. We should never forget to thank God for the fact that our hearts are beating, our lungs are dilating and even for the fact that our bowels are behaving. If we are in good health, we should thank God for it. One day we shall all know what it is like not to be fit. One day we shall nearly all of us grow ill and die.

Connected with this is the blessing of physical healing. Sometimes God is pleased to heal people physically and this is always a great cause of thanksgiving. I recall a recent incident in which my wife Alie was lying awake in bed, in agony because of a severe viral infection. We had called the doctor and there had been no improvement. Eventually, more in desperation than in faith (though desperation can be a very deep kind of faith), I laid my hands on her and prayed a short and not very believing prayer: 'In the name of Jesus, be healed and sleep well!' Within a few seconds she was asleep. The next morning she was completely healed. There was a lot of thanking God in our household the next day.

Counting our physical blessings is therefore partly about health and healing. But there are other aspects of our bodies for which we need to give thanks. We need to learn to give thanks for the way God has made us. Our body-image should not be influenced by the media's cosmetic understanding of physical shapeliness. Our body-image should be influenced by the Word of God. From Scriptures like Psalm 139 we need to remember that God designed our bodies in our mothers' wombs. As far as God is concerned, whatever we look like physically we are fearfully and wonderfully made. God made our bodies and we should therefore thank him for them.

Connected with this is the issue of our sexuality. Again, the biblical expression of our sexuality is something to be enjoyed and

26

celebrated. It is a cause for thanksgiving. Sexual intercourse within marriage is therefore not something shameful, but rather a beautiful and exciting gift of God. If we are blessed enough to be married, let us therefore not hold back from thanking God for the play and intimacy of sexual love. Let us not be Gnostic in our thinking and relegate such matters to the dirty, the ungodly and the evil. Such experiences should form part of the regular repertoire of our gratitude.

Emotional blessings

If physical blessings are to be appreciated, so are emotional blessings. Anything which brings joy to our hearts should be the cause of thanksgiving. The joy of a kiss, the joy of a sunset, the joy of a compliment, the joy of a child's first steps, the joy of inner healing: all these can provide us with a heightened sense of gratitude. Anything that touches, enlivens and blesses our emotions can become the stimulus for thanksgiving. Anything which helps us to live life more abundantly, more playfully, more ecstatically can make us thankful. Such moments of plenitude can form the content of *berakah* prayer.

Earlier in this chapter I referred to Zechariah, the father of John the Baptist. It is lovely to note that when his baby boy was eventually born, he too uttered a *berakah* to God:

> Blessed be the Lord, the God of Israel, because he has come and redeemed his people. He has raised up a horn of salvation for us in the house of his servant David (as he said through his holy prophets of long ago), salvation from our enemies and from the hand of all who hate us – to show mercy to our fathers and to remember his holy covenant, the oath he swore to our father Abraham: to rescue us from the hand of our enemies and to enable us to serve him without fear in holiness and righteousness before him all our days.

At this point, overwhelmed with emotion at the impossible miracle of his son's birth, Zechariah turns from addressing God to addressing his baby boy:

And you, my child, will be called a prophet of the Most High; for you will go on before the Lord to prepare the way for him, to give his people the knowledge of salvation through the forgiveness of their sins, because of the tender mercy of our God, by which the rising sun will come to us from heaven, to shine on those living in darkness and the shadow of death, to guide our feet into the path of peace (Luke 1.68–79).

Like Zechariah, we can thank God for emotional blessings.

Intellectual blessings

The same goes for intellectual blessings. Our minds can be a great barrier to God but they can also be the *locus* of tremendous revelation and pleasure. Those times when we feel as though our minds have been stimulated, enriched and ennobled are occasions of thanksgiving, whether the stimulus to that enrichment was a secular novel or an anointed sermon. Such times should again be seen as treasures given by the Spirit of God.

People tend to be, by temperament, either analytical or artistic – rarely both. When I speak of counting our intellectual blessings I am thinking of giving thanks for those things which give pleasure at either the analytical or the artistic level. Those whose thinking is dominated by mathematical or philosophical leanings may be blessed by an equation or a maxim. Those whose thinking is dominated by more artistic leanings may derive pleasure from a landscape or a poem. Whatever is true, whatever is noble, whatever is right, whatever is pure, whatever is lovely, whatever is admirable – if anything is excellent or praiseworthy – think about such things (Philippians 4.8). Think about them and thank God for them.

Material blessings

We should learn also to thank God for his provision of material and financial blessings. For most of us, God has provided a roof over our heads and a home for us to live in. Even if that home will never belong to some of us, we still have a place to sleep, eat, wash and keep warm in. In a world where these kind of things are denied to so many, there is a real need for us to learn gratitude. We must grow to be thankful for toothpaste and toilets, for baths and for basins.

Thanking God for material blessings does not mean advocating what has been called a 'prosperity gospel'. Many Christian leaders in the West are teaching that the blessings given to Abraham, which include material prosperity, can be claimed through faith by today's Christians. I do not concur with that view. Anyone who looks at the life of Jesus and indeed of the first Christians is struck not by a prosperity gospel but by an *austerity* gospel. He or she is struck by the fact of God's gracious provision for our basic needs on the one hand, but also by a call to a simple lifestyle on the other.

This does not, of course, mean an end to feasting and fun. Far from it. The Christian life is celebration. That is why Jesus begins his ministry in John's Gospel with the miraculous transformation of about 180 gallons of water into heavenly wine. That signifies to me that the new age of the Spirit, which we are still living in, is an age of joy and festival.

However, the terrible deprivation and degradation of the world's unemployed, hungry, bereaved and destitute will mean that we who bear the name of Christ will also want to set boundaries on spending and feasting. We will want to offer up a constant *berakah* for the way God meets our basic needs, and for those times when he permits us to revel and to play. We will not be a prosperity people but a grateful, disciplined people.

Relational blessings
Let us remember, finally, to count our relational blessings, the blessings which we receive from our relationships with others.

There are a number of relationships which give me cause for gratitude. First of all, there are those friends who give me the freedom to be myself. In my experience, this is one of the greatest joys: 'to be free to be me'. In my profession as a clergyman, I find that there are many expectations of how I should behave and what I should or should not say. Many of these expectations are right. But the effect of them is that they sometimes force me into a state of unnatural self-vigilance, making it virtually impossible to relax completely.

However, the friends who delight in the real me, rather than the professional me, are a real blessing. They are people for whom I give thanks. An evening meal, a game of snooker, a brief telephone call with friends like these are occasional but much appreciated. They are immensely important for one's wholeness and sanity.

Secondly, there are our families. I am blessed to have a wife and children. My personal testimony is this: that I feel called to offer up a *berakah* for my marriage and my family life *every day*. I feel called to express my gratitude for the relationships within my own home: for the children with their vitality, laughter and health; for my wife, with her beauty, gifts and love. None of them is to be taken for granted. All are a precious gift of God's abundant grace.

Thirdly, there are Christian brothers and sisters whom we meet and with whom, so often, we strike up a mysteriously quick accord. This, like the gift of true friends and family, is also a gift of grace. When Paul says to his Christian brothers and sisters in Philippi, 'I thank my God every time I remember you' (Philippians 1.3), he was speaking with a note of profound gratitude and sincere affection. He was speaking as one who knew the importance of counting relational blessings in prayer.

Occasions of Thanksgiving

So we have looked at spiritual, physical, emotional, intellectual, material and relational blessings. When the Scripture says, 'Out of the fullness of God's grace, God has given us all one blessing after another', these are the kinds of blessings which we need to remember in thankfulness. The gates of thanksgiving loom large before us. But they are easily passed through *berakah* prayer.

How much time, then, should be spent on such thanksgiving? On a daily basis, between two and ten minutes should be adequate. This is simply because the amount of time we are reviewing is usually limited to twenty-four hours. Usually we will be looking back over the previous day and night, so the amount for which we can give thanks is finite. However, there are some occasions in the year when it is good to spend much longer in thanksgiving, indeed when it is right to spend the majority of time in this *eucharistic*, priestly ministry.

Longer periods of thanksgiving are important at the end of every week. On a Sunday morning we can look back over the previous week and thank God for those things which the Spirit brings to remembrance. On our birthday it is good to look back over the whole year. The same is true for a wedding anniversary, or for New Year's Eve. Do not forget your spiritual birthday either: if you know the date when you were converted, use that day as a day of thanksgiving. Thank God for leading you to where you are right now. Thank him for those who led you to Christ and who have made an impact on you since.

There are consequently some set occasions for a special ministry of thanksgiving. The most important occasions of all, however, are not anniversaries but seasons of tribulation or dryness. I honestly believe that the ability to thank God for some of the negative experiences of our lives is as important, if not more important, than the ability to thank him for all the positive things which we have discussed so far. It is easy to thank God when the going is easy. It is much harder, of course, when we are under stress. But the ability to thank God in the hard times is actually a deep sign of trust.

There is a lovely story in the Jewish Talmud which illustrates the basis for this kind of trust. There we read:

> Rabbi Huna said . . . A person should develop the habit of saying always: 'Everything that God does he does for a good purpose.' On one occasion when Rabbi Aqiba was on a journey, he came to a town and asked for hospitality, but did not receive it; he then said, 'Everything that God does he does for a purpose.' He went off and spent the night in the open. He had with him a cock, an ass and a lantern. The wind arose and extinguished the lantern: a cat came and ate the cock; a lion came and ate the ass. Yet he said, 'Everything God does he does for a purpose.' During the night, invading troops came and took the townspeople prisoner; and he said, 'Did I not tell you: Everything that God does for a purpose?'[11]

The basis for gratitude in adverse circumstances is the fact that God is sovereign, and so all things ultimately work to the good for those who love him. Thanking God when times are hard is a sure sign that we trust that '*Everything* that God does he does for a purpose'. With that in mind, we can more easily obey Paul when he writes, 'Give thanks (*eucharisteite*) in all circumstances, for this is God's will for you in Christ Jesus' (1 Thessalonians 5.18).

One of Our Best Words

So we should not underestimate the power of gratitude. It is said that when Rudyard Kipling was writing at his prime, he received a shilling for every word that he wrote for one particular newspaper. Some undergraduates at Oxford University heard about this and, as a ruse, sent Kipling a shilling, and asked him to send them one of his best words. Immediately Kipling cabled back a one-word answer to the students: 'Thanks!'

'Thanks' is one of our best words as Christians.

PRAYER

Almighty God, I want now to enter your gates with thanksgiving. Please lead me, as a priest of your kingdom, into an authentic eucharistic ministry. Help me to overflow with thankfulness.

I want to begin by thanking you that out of the fullness of your grace, you have given me one blessing after another. Help me now to count my beads of gracious moments. Help me to savour all those ways in which you have helped me to enjoy life in all its fullness.

Lord I thank you for the following spiritual blessings over the last twenty-four hours . . .

Lord I thank you for all the physical blessings too . . .

Thank you for those moments when you have touched my emotions . . .

Thank you for the following material blessings . . .

Thank you for feeding my mind . . .

And thank you for the relationships which I have been privileged to enjoy since we last met in this way . . .

Thank you, Father. Amen.

2
THE COURT OF PRAISE

*'Man need never be so defeated that he cannot do anything.
Weak, sick, broken in body, far from home, and alone in
a strange land, he can sing! He can worship!'*
Ernest Gordon, *Miracle on the River Kwai*

The first stage of prayer is now complete. We have looked back over the time since we last prayed, and given voice to our gratitude for what God has done for us. As we have done so, the gates of God's holy presence have opened wide, revealing the inner court in which the great sanctuary was situated. This is the court of praise. It is a place of adoration.

The Court of Praise

Before we examine the actual practice of praise, we need to look in more detail at this inner court. According to most scholars there were two main courts in the Temple area. There was first of all the outer court, sometimes called the court of the Gentiles. This area, paved with flagstones and mosaics, could be entered by anyone. A little to the west was a stairway which you had to climb in order to reach the terrace on which the sanctuary was built. This raised area was an inner court also known as the court of the priests. Whereas anyone could enter the court of the Gentiles, only priests could climb the stairway and enter the raised inner court.

It is this raised inner court of which the psalmist often speaks. It is this area of the Temple for which he longs:

> My soul yearns, even faints,
>> for the courts of the Lord;
> my heart and my flesh cry out
>> for the living God.
> Even the sparrow has found a home,
>> and the swallow a nest for herself,
>> where she may have her young –
> a place near your altar,
>> O Lord Almighty, my King and my God. (Psalm 84.2–4).

The reason why the psalmist longs to be in this upper court is because it is the place of ongoing praise and adoration of God. In Psalm 135.1–2 he declares:

Praise the Lord.
Praise the name of the Lord;
  praise him, you servants of the Lord,
you who minister in the house of the Lord,
  in the courts of the house of our God.

In this outburst of enthusiasm the writer calls upon the priests on duty in the inner courts to praise God with extravagant devotion. As he goes on, 'Praise the Lord, for the Lord is good; sing praise to his name for that is pleasant'.

So when the writer of Psalm 100 says, 'Enter his gates with thanksgiving and his courts with praise', we can understand him to be asking the people of God to spend time not only thanking God for what he has done, but also to proceed beyond that, to a higher level of worship, in which heartfelt praise is offered for God's infinite and unfathomable nature.

The Nature of Praise

In the last chapter I outlined the time-honoured distinction between thanksgiving and praise. Thanksgiving is about God's acts. Praise is about God's being. In thanksgiving we express our gratitude for what God has done for us. In praising God we worship him for who he is.

This distinction is important in practice. My experience of open prayer suggests that we are much better at thanking God than we are at praising him. Whenever a leader says, 'Let's praise God', it is amazing how often what follows is, in reality, thanksgiving. We launch with enthusiasm and eloquence into thanking God for the Cross, for healing, for answered prayer, and so on. In the process, we do not realize that, strictly speaking, we have misunderstood the directive. The leader said, 'Let us praise!' not 'Let us thank!'

The Poverty of Praise

One of the reasons why we find it so hard to praise is because of the limitations of our language. Deep down we recognize that our

36

finite vocabulary is insufficient to describe God's infinite nature. So when we are encouraged to praise God, we all of us hesitate and feel a bit lost. How on earth are we going to find the words to express sincere awe at a God who is in heaven? How are we going to praise him without either sounding pious or superficial? At least in the area of thanksgiving we are dealing with things that we can see and touch. But with praise, that is a different matter altogether. Here we are attempting to bridge that enormous, metaphysical gap between ourselves and the one who is immortal and invisible.

So one reason behind the poverty of our praise in public worship lies with our vocabulary. Another has to do with our own, personal prayer life. The fact is that the corporate is always an expression of the private. Put another way, how we pray in public is a very good indication of how we pray on our own. One of the main reasons for the poverty of praise in public has to do with a poverty of praise in our private devotion. For many of us it is true to say that our prayer life is far more preoccupied with who we are than who God is. Far more time is given to confession, often with a suggestion of negative self-absorption, than to adoration.

The Importance of Praise

Today we need to improve the quality of our praise. Praise is, quite simply, vital. It is vital, first of all, to God. God loves to hear us praise him for specific aspects of his character. He does not love to hear our praise for the reasons we love praise. In other words, he does not crave adoration because his ego needs boosting, or because his heart needs affirming. God has no such unmet needs or insecurities. God loves to hear our praise because it shows him that we are taking every part of his nature seriously. It shows him that we desire to understand and value him, however far short of total comprehension this will inevitably fall.

To illustrate this, look at the analogy of human relationships. If you were to ask my wife Alie which she preferred, thanksgiving or

37

praise, she would probably reply, 'I like both, but I prefer being praised'. If I say 'Thank you for that lovely meal', that gives Alie pleasure because it shows her that I have not taken her hard work for granted. But if I say, 'Alie, I think you're the most creative person I know', that gives her even greater pleasure. It shows her that I love her for who she is, and not for what she does for me.

So it is with God. God loves to hear us praise him for all the multi-faceted qualities of his character. He longs to know that we love him for who he is and not for what we can get out of him. Too many relationships today are the product of 'utilitarian individualism'. In other words, they exist because we can get something out of the other person. This is not to be true of our relationship with God. God is not a 'credit-card deity' whom we can access for our own needs. He is the One, True Living God in whom we live and move and have our being. A healthy diet of praise each day keeps us from appreciating God only for what he gives us.

The Benefits of Praise

If praise is important to God, it is consequently important to us. Our spiritual health depends largely upon us spending time each day gazing with devotion upon God's being.

This came home to me with particular force when I was asked to minister to a man who was suffering from depression. He had received a lot of counselling but it produced little fruit. When I started helping him I had no idea what to do but I did feel burdened to take him back to basics: I began to relay the foundations of his faith by talking about the essentials of discipleship and by gently challenging him on each of these.

Not surprisingly this did not help very much. It drove him deeper into guilt and left me with the distinct impression that we were getting nowhere. However, one day we had a breakthrough. We started looking at aspects of God's nature, focusing initially upon his fatherly love, then upon his holiness, and so on. As soon as this happened, my friend's eyes lit up. He seemed to come alive. Indeed, I can remember his words, 'Now *this* is really helpful. It's a lot more healthy concentrating upon God than upon me. Let's run with this approach for a while'.

What God was teaching me was the healing power of praise. Through praise, we stop staring downwards at the shadow of our hurts and sins (which are enough to depress many of us) and we start to look upwards at a much more soul-affirming reality, the beauty of God's heart. As Teresa of Avila once put it:

> Self-knowledge is necessary,
> no matter how high the state of the soul,
> and we must never neglect it.
> Humility must ever be doing its work
> like a bee making honey in the hive;
> without humility all is lost.
> But sometimes
> the soul must emerge from self-knowledge
> and soar aloft in meditation
> on the greatness and majesty of its God.
> Thus it will realize its own baseness
> rather than in thinking about itself.
> *We shall reach much greater heights of virtue*
> *by thinking of the virtue of God*
> *than if we stay in our own little plot of ground*
> *and tie ourselves down to it completely* (my italics).[1]

The Power of Praise

One person who discovered this truth and expressed it with conviction was the poet John Milton. He was a man who had good cause for introspection and depression. He went blind, a severe handicap to a man who dearly wanted to serve God as a poet. One of his most poignant poems is about his spiritual journey from confusion to acceptance. It is simply called, 'On his blindness'.

Milton's poem is a sonnet. A sonnet is a carefully constructed poem of fourteen lines, in which very often the first eight lines portray a problem, and the final six lines present some kind of solution, usually beginning with the word 'But'. Milton's sonnet is no exception. In the first eight lines, Milton laments the loss of his sight before he is halfway through the course of his life. He laments that his eyesight is now hidden, like a talent, and that his eyes are now lodged in their sockets as useless organs. He then wonders whether God will hold him to account for not serving him as other, non-handicapped people can:

> When *I* consider how *my* light is spent
> Ere half *my* days, in this dark world and wide,
> And that one talent which is death to hide,
> Lodg'd with *me* useless, though *my* soul more bent
> To serve therewith *my* Maker, and present
> *My* true account, lest he returning chide;
> 'Doth God exact day-labour, light denied,'
> *I* fondly ask:

In these eight lines, the most noticeable feature of the language is the emphasis upon the self. I have put all the first person pronouns in italics so as to highlight the degree of self-preoccupation and self-doubt which Milton clearly felt. What is so striking in the second half of the poem is the transition from 'self-centred' language to 'God-centred' language. The way out of Milton's depression occurs when he moves from an emphasis upon 'me' to an emphasis upon 'him' (i.e. God):

>   But Patience, to prevent
> That murmur, soon replies, '*God* doth not need
> Either man's work, or *his* own gifts; who best
> Bear *his* mild yoke, they serve *him* best: *his* state
> Is kingly; thousands at *his* bidding speed,
> And post o'er land and ocean without rest;
> They also serve who only stand and wait.

Milton's sonnet is therefore a testimony to emotional healing. In the first eight lines he is preoccupied with himself and with his blindness. In the second part of the poem he decides to become preoccupied with God. Instead of going deeper into himself, Milton chooses to dwell upon God's goodness. From the eighth line onwards, there are therefore no more references to 'I', to 'me', but only to 'God', to 'him', to 'he'. This enables Milton to close his sonnet with a beautiful statement of assurance. Having focused upon God's 'kingly state', he declares that 'They also serve who only stand and wait'. Even those whose disabilities necessitate a more passive role are authentic servants of God.

This poem is a beautiful example of the way in which the power of praise can liberate us from toxic introspection. As C.S. Lewis once put it, 'Praise almost seems to be inner health made audible'. Praise is the audible consequence of a soul whose gaze is turned upwards rather than inwards.

The Practice of Praise

Given the poverty of our language, how can we best praise God? The first thing to realize is that God has given us a wonderful thesaurus of praise in the Scriptures where he has taken hold of our frail and finite vocabulary and invested it with a capacity for true revelation. So one of the ways through the language barrier is to take hold of the Scriptures which are adorational in character and to use them as the basis of our own worship.

The psalms are a particularly helpful resource in this respect. These songs are, in all probability, the hymns which were sung in the Temple of God's presence.

Scholars have divided the praise psalms into those which are descriptive and those which are declarative. The descriptive psalms describe the great things which God has done while the declarative psalms tend to rejoice in who God is. The descriptive psalms are therefore an aid to thanksgiving (which addresses God's deeds) while the declarative psalms are an aid to praise (which addresses God's being).

41

One example of a declarative psalm is Psalm 30.4–5:

> Sing to the Lord, you saints of his;
> > praise his holy name.
> For his anger lasts only a moment,
> > but his favour lasts a lifetime;
> Weeping may return for a night,
> > but rejoicing comes in the morning!

Within these two verses, there is some very powerful language of praise. Notice the words 'anger' and 'favour', which perfectly capture those two aspects of God's nature which we often describe as 'justice' and 'love'. 'Anger' and 'favour' are beautiful synonyms for 'justice' and 'love'. They could easily form the basis of personal praise:

> O Lord God, I praise you for your holy anger, a side of your nature I often choose to neglect. I praise you that you are holy, that you are justly angered by my sins. But I praise you even more because your anger lasts only a moment, while your favour lasts a lifetime. Praise you for your favour, Lord.

Praising the Name of the Lord

This practice of praying back the Scriptures which are adorational in character is one of the most powerful spiritual disciplines, both in private and public prayer. Too often we treat Scripture as information when it is often declaration. The devotional exclamations of the psalms can bring great blessing to our spirit if we turn them back into that purpose for which many of them were originally designed: devotion.

One emphasis which we often find in the psalms is on the name of the Lord. Praising the Lord for his 'name' is a frequent characteristic of the declarative psalms. The psalm which we have just examined exhorts us to 'praise his holy name' (30.4). The greatest of these names is 'Jehovah' or 'Yahweh', which David

THE COURT OF PRAISE

Pawson has translated as 'Always'. This translation helps us to use God's name in personal praise:

> Jehovah Roi   Always my Shepherd
> Jehovah Jireh   Always my Provider
> Jehovah Nissi   Always my Banner
> Jehovah Shalom   Always my Peace
> Jehovah Shammah Always There
> Jehovah Tsidkenu Always my Righteousness
> Jehovah M'Kaddesh Always my Holiness
> Jehovah Rapha   Always my Healer

No wonder the psalmist tells us to praise God's holy name (30.4; 69.30; 96.2; 145.21; 148.13).

The Praise of High Christology

If it is important to praise the name of the Lord using the Old Testament Scriptures, how much more important is it to praise him using the language of the New Testament. In the New Testament there are many new names or titles given to Jesus, the Son of God. I have found it very helpful to take these names and to use them in what I call 'the praise of high Christology'.

What then is high Christology? Christology is our understanding of the person and significance of Jesus Christ. All of us, as Christians, have a Christology. Liberal Christians tend to have a 'low' Christology, an understanding of Jesus as a moral teacher, the embodiment of love, a window on to God. Such phrases stop far short of saying that Jesus was the unique Son of God, the Messiah, the Risen and Ascended Lord. This second kind of understanding is usually embraced by more conservative Christians, especially those who believe that the Bible is the authoritative Word of God. This second position would be termed a 'high Christology'.

My personal conviction is that a high Christology is the only Christology which makes sense of the biblical evidence and of the Church's experience of Jesus. Marcus Borg, a fine New Testament scholar, has recently written a widely acclaimed work entitled

Jesus. A New Vision, which begins with these powerful words about Jesus:

> No other figure in the history of the West has ever been accorded such extraordinary status. Within a few decades of his death, stories were told of his miraculous birth. By the end of the first century, he was extolled with the most exalted titles known within the religious tradition out of which he came: Son of God, one with the Father, the Word become flesh, the bread of life, the light of the world, the one who would come again as cosmic judge and Lord. Within a few centuries he had become Lord of the empire which had crucified him.

As if this was not impressive enough, Borg goes on to highlight the towering supremacy and influence of Jesus on the rest of history:

> For over a thousand years thereafter, he dominated the culture of the West: its religion and devotion, its art, music, and architecture, its intellectual thought and ethical norms, even its politics. Our calendar affirms his life as a dividing point in world history. On historical grounds alone, with no convictions of faith shaping the verdict, Jesus is the most important figure in Western (and perhaps human) history.[2]

These words show from the evidence of history that Jesus is worthy of the highest honour. Combine this with the evidence of Scripture, and the evidence of our personal experience, and we have good grounds for celebrating the ultimacy of Jesus. 'High Christology' should therefore form the true content of our praise in the court of the priests!

The Erosion of High Christology

The reason why this is so important is because there has been a slow and destructive erosion of high Christology in the Christian Church over the course of this century. Two factors in particular have contributed to this.

First of all, it cannot be denied that liberal theology has significantly influenced the widespread loss of nerve concerning the deity of Jesus. In particular, German biblical scholarship since the beginning of the twentieth century has consistently contended that Jesus never claimed to be the Messiah. Many scholars argued that this belief was written into the gospels by the early church. Rudolf Bultmann, who claimed that all high Christology in the gospels is redactional (i.e. superimposed on to the teaching of the historical Jesus) is perhaps the most famous example of this position.

The ramifications of this scholarship for the life of the Church should not be ignored. The majority of people training in theological and Bible colleges since the Second World War have been exposed to this hermeneutic of scepticism. This has produced a large number of ministers who have adopted the liberal position associated mainly with German scholarship. The most outspoken of these in recent times has been Bishop David Jenkins, who is on record as saying that the virgin birth was invented by the early church, and that one can no longer be certain about anything which the New Testament says.

Theological liberalism has therefore produced a portrait of Jesus in which the elements pertaining to his uniqueness and his deity have been stripped away. But there has been a second cause for concern of late, one which is probably not unconnected to this Christological liberalism. This second corrosive factor has been the emergence of a confusing religious pluralism. There are many religious cults today which masquerade as Christian and yet which contain a very low Christology at best, and at worst a view of Jesus based on nothing short of deception. These movements are also influencing the Church, the academy and society as a whole.

Most obvious are the large number of religious beliefs which have been subsumed under the label, the New Age. It is difficult to talk precisely about such an amorphous movement, but one common denominator seems to be a highly deceptive and erroneous view of Jesus. On the surface of it, New Agers appear to have the highest of all Christologies. They speak of the Christ Spirit, and of the Cosmic Christ who pervades the universe. However, close inspection reveals that this is just a cover-up for a very destructive view of Jesus.

Thus, for example, New Agers do not believe in the virgin birth. In his book *Truth Vibrations*, David Icke writes that 'Jesus was the only child of Mary and Joseph and he was not the result of a "virgin birth". Jesus was born Jeshua-ben-Josephus on September 19 in the constellation of Virgo, the virgin, and this helped to fuel the myth of the virgin birth'. What, then, of Jesus' death and resurrection? The same writer argues: 'Jesus did not die . . . so that all our sins could be forgiven. That is for us to do through the law of karma. . . . The resurrection of the physical body of Jesus is another myth. . . . In reality his body went back to the earth like all other bodies do. . . . Friends buried the body in a cellar and it has never been found'.[3]

The Importance of Christology

The two streams of liberalism and pluralism have contributed to a gradual sense of uncertainty in the Church's worship and evangelism. This stands to reason if we think about it for a moment: how can we worship Jesus as the Lord of all when modern trends of thought are arguing that he was never Lord at all? How can we share the Good News about Jesus if we have been taken in by so much bad news about him?

I want to suggest in this chapter that we need to spend time praying back to God those Scriptures which use exalted names and titles for Jesus. Biblical passages which contain a high Christology should be the content of our praise in the second stage of prayer. Peter, in his first letter, commands us, 'in your hearts, set apart Christ as Lord' (1 Peter 3.15); in other words, 'Develop the regular discipline of exalting Jesus with heartfelt praise'. He then goes on to add, 'Always be prepared to give an answer to everyone who asks you to give the reason for the hope that you have' (1 Peter 3.15).

The second of these statements, 'Always be ready to give a defence', and the first of these statements, 'Set apart Christ as Lord', are not unconnected remarks: they are logically related. Indeed, the first command constitutes a cause, and the second its effect. The more we set apart Christ as Lord in our hearts (through prayers of praise), the more ready we shall be to provide a reasoned and cogent defence of our hope (through evangelism). The more we fill our hearts with praise for the Lord Jesus, the more fluently our mouths will utter truths concerning the ultimacy of the Lord Jesus.

The Names of Jesus

There are many names and titles for Jesus in the New Testament. I find it helpful to pray using an A to Z of his names. This is a practice which has quite a history in evangelical circles and is, I believe, enormously beneficial.[4] Many people have remarked to me how the A to Z of Jesus' names has given them a whole new lease of life in the court of praise.

The following is an A to Z of Jesus' New Testament names which can be used in the court of praise.

A   Advocate with the Father (1 John 2.1)
     Alpha (Revelation 22.13)
     The Amen (Revelation 3.14)
     Apostle whom we Confess (Hebrews 3.1)
     The Atoning Sacrifice (1 John 2.2)
     Author of Life (Acts 3.15)
     Author of Our Salvation (Hebrews 2.10)
     Author of Our Faith (Hebrews 12.2)

B   Beginning (Revelation 22.13)
     Beloved (Ephesians 1.6)
     Beloved Son (Matthew 3.17)
     Blameless One (Hebrews 7.26)
     Bread of God (John 6.33)
     Bread of Life (John 6.35)
     Bridegroom (John 3.29)
     Bright Morning Star (Revelation 22.16)

C   Capstone (1 Peter 2.7)
     Chief Cornerstone (Ephesians 2.20; 1 Peter 2.6)
     Chief Shepherd (1 Peter 5.4)

Chosen by God (1 Peter 2.4)
Christ
The Christ
The Christ of God
Christ Jesus
Christ Jesus the Lord
Christ the Lord
Christ our Passover Lamb (1 Corinthians 5.7)
Consolation of Israel (Luke 2.25)

D Descendant of David (Romans 1.3)
Door of the Sheep (John 10.7)

E Emmanuel (Matthew 1.23)
Eternal Life (1 John 5.20)
Exact Representation of God (Hebrews 1.3)
Exalted above the Heavens (Hebrews 7.26)

F Faithful (1 Thessalonians 5.24)
Faithful and True (Revelation 19.11)
Faithful Witness (lit. 'Martyr': Revelation 1.5)
Faithful High Priest (Hebrews 2.17)
First (Revelation 22.13)
Firstborn (Hebrews 1.6; 12.23)
Firstborn among many Brothers (Romans 8.29)
Firstborn from the Dead (Revelation 1.5)
Firstborn over all Creation (Colossians 1.15)
First Fruits of those who have Fallen Asleep (1 Corinthians
    15.20)
Foundation (1 Corinthians 3.11)
Fragrant Offering (Ephesians 5.2)
Friend of Sinners (Luke 7.34)

G Glory of the One and Only (John 1.14)
God Over All (Romans 8.5)
God With Us (Matthew 1.23)
Good Shepherd (John 10.11)

48

Great God (Titus 2.13)
Great High Priest (Hebrews 4.14)
Great Shepherd of the Sheep (Hebrews 13.20)
Greater than Abraham (John 8.53)
Greater than Jacob (John 4.12)
Greater than Jonah (Matthew 12.41)
Greater than Solomon (Matthew 12.42)
Greater than the Temple (Matthew 12.6)

H   Head over Every Power and Authority (Colossians 2.10)
Head of Every Man (1 Corinthians 11.3)
Head of the Body, the Church (Colossians 1.18)
Heir of All Things (Hebrews 1.2)
High Priest (Hebrews 5.5)
High Priest after the Order of Melchizedek (Hebrews 5.10)
High Priest forever (Hebrews 6.20)
Holy One (Acts 2.27)
Holy One of God (John 6.69)
Holy and Righteous One (Acts 3.14)
Holy Servant (Acts 4.27)
Our Hope (1 Timothy 1.1)
Hope of Glory (Colossians 1.27)
Hope of Israel (Acts 28.20)
Horn of Salvation (Luke 1.69)

I   I Am (John 8.28)
Image of the Invisible God (Colossians 1.15)
The Innocent One (Matthew 12.7)

J   Jesus
Jesus Christ
Jesus Christ the Lord
Jesus Christ, the Son of God
Jesus of Galilee
Jesus of Nazareth
Judge of the Living and the Dead (Acts 10.42)

K   Kindness and Love of God (Titus 3.4)
King of Israel (John 1.49)
King of Kings (Revelation 19.16)
King of Peace (Hebrews 7.2)
King of Righteousness (Hebrews 7.2)

L   Lamb (Revelation 17.14)
Lamb of God (John 1.29)
Lamb that was Slain from the Creation of the World
(Revelation 13.8)
The Lamb who was Slain (Revelation 5.12)
Last (Revelation 22.13)
The Last Adam (1 Corinthians 15.45)
Life (John 14.6)
Light (John 1.7)
Light of Men (John 1.4)
Light of the World (John 8.12)
Light for Revelation to the Gentiles (Luke 2.32)
Lion of Judah (Revelation 5.5)
Living Bread (John 6.51)
Lord
Lord of the Sabbath (Mark 2.28)
Lord and Saviour (2 Peter 1.11)
Lord of Both the Dead and the Living (Romans 14.9)
The Lord of Glory (1 Corinthians 2.8)
Lord of Lords (Revelation 19.16)

M   Man (Behold the Man! John 19.5)
A Man Accredited by God (Acts 2.22)
The Man Christ Jesus (1 Timothy 2.5)
The Man God has Appointed (Acts 17.31)
Mediator (1 Timothy 2.5)
Mediator of a new covenant (Hebrews 12.24)
Merciful (Hebrews 2.17)
Morning Star (2 Peter 1.19)
Mystery of God (Colossians 2.2)

N Name Above Every Name (Philippians 2.9)

O Offering (Ephesians 5.2)
Offspring of David (Revelation 22.16)
Omega (Revelation 22.13)
The One and Only (John 1.14, 3.16)

P Our Peace (Ephesians 2.14)
Perfecter of Our Faith (Hebrews 12.2)
Power of God (1 Corinthians 1.24)
Prince and Saviour (Acts 5.31)
Prophet, Powerful in Word and Deed (Luke 24.19)

R Radiance of God's Glory (Hebrews 1.3)
Ransom for All Men (1 Timothy 2.6)
Ransom for Many (Mark 10.45)
Redemption (1 Corinthians 1.30)
Resurrection (John 11.25)
Righteous Judge (2 Timothy 4.8)
Righteous One (Acts 7.52; 1 John 2.1)
Rising Sun (Luke 1.78)
Root of David (Revelation 5.5)
Ruler of the Kings of the Earth (Revelation 1.5)

S Sacrifice to God (Ephesians 5.2)
Salvation (Luke 2.30)
Saviour (Titus 2.13)
Saviour of the Body, the Church (Ephesians 5.10)
Saviour of the World (John 4.42)
Second Adam (1 Corinthians 15.46–7)
Shepherd and Overseer of our Souls (1 Peter 2.25)
The Son
Son of Abraham (Matthew 1.1)
Son of Adam (Luke 3.38)
Son of the Blessed One (Mark 14.61)
Son of David (Matthew 1.1)
Son of the Father (2 John 3)

Son of God
Son of the Living God (Matthew 16.16)
Son of Man
Son of the Most High (Luke 1.32)
Supreme (Colossians 1.18)

T   Teacher Come from God (John 3.2)
    True Vine (John 15.1)
    The Truth (John 14.6)

U   Unknown God (Acts 17.23)

V   Vine (John 15.1)

W   Way (John 14.6)
    Wisdom of God (1 Corinthians 1.24)
    The Word (John 1.1)
    The Word of Life (1 John 1.1)
    The Worthy One (Revelation 5.12)

Y   The Yes of God (2 Corinthians 1.18–20)

Using the Names in Prayer

There are really three ways of using this A to Z of Christology.
First of all, you can meditate on one name and worship Jesus using
that. For example, today I concentrated on Jesus as 'The One and
Only of God'. Having done a bit of research using the commentaries, I discovered that the Greek word translated 'One and Only' is
monogenes. This means 'of a single (*monos*) kind (*genos*)' or
'unique'. This in turn is almost certainly a Greek form of the
Hebrew word *yahid* meaning 'only, precious', a word used in
Genesis 22.2, 12, 16 of Abraham's son Isaac ('your son, your only
son').

With that piece of information in my mind I turned to the three
New Testament texts which use this description of Jesus:

John 1.14 We have seen his glory, the glory of the One and Only, who came from the Father, full of grace and truth.

John 1.18 No one has ever seen God, but God the One and Only, who is at the Father's side, has made him known.

John 3.16 For God so loved the world that he gave his One and Only Son, that whoever believes in him shall not perish but have eternal life.

Using the language of these verses, I was able to praise Jesus for the fact that he is the One and Only One, the unique and infinitely precious Son of God, who is full of glory, grace, truth, revelation and life. Using just one of the many titles in the A to Z above, I was able to soar to new heights in prayers of praise.

The second way of praising Jesus is either to take all the titles under one letter and pray through those, or to take one title from each letter and just start with A and proceed to Z. However, you may have to do some research concerning the full significance of some of these titles if they are to yield their true significance. The example above ('One and Only') shows that there are great depths in many of these Christological names.

The third way of using this list involves praying to God those names for Jesus which have greatest relevance to the Temple. There is much in the letter to the Hebrews which helps us to worship Jesus in language reminiscent of the Temple. Why not try using Hebrews 4.14–5.10 as your principal resource for praise? These magnificent words describe Jesus as the Great High Priest who has gone through the heavens, who is able to sympathize with our weaknesses, who has opened up the way to God's throne, who was anointed high priest by God Himself, high priest in the order of Melchizedek. You can also use Hebrews 7.11–10.18 in a similar way to praise Jesus for having opened up the sanctuary of heaven, and for having given you access to the most holy place of God's presence. These chapters are among the most worshipful in the entire Bible.

The prayer of the mind

So what are the virtues of this kind of praise? First of all, this kind of praise is *biblical*. Recently a number of prominent Christian writers have been complaining that the evangelical world has lost a sense of its roots in the area of spirituality. This complaint is not unjustified. Some evangelical books on prayer resort to the Orthodox, Catholic and mystical traditions in order to promote a more creative approach to the 'daily quiet time with God'. In doing so, their evangelicalism becomes almost invisible. However, praise Christology relies more on Scripture than on the saints for its inspiration. As the description above should have demonstrated, it is a biblical discipline. It draws from the well of Scripture at every point.

Secondly, this kind of praise is *theological*, it is prayer 'with the mind'. Paul reminds us of the need to engage our mental faculties in worship when he writes 'I will pray with my spirit but I will also pray with my mind; I will sing with my spirit but I will also sing with my mind' (1 Corinthians 14.15). One of the virtues of using high Christology is that it does make our prayer life more theological. This kind of praise renews the mind.

This is vital. It was Karl Barth who often said that theology should become more prayerful.[5] He pointed to Anselm's *Proslogion*, a great theological work couched entirely in the form of worshipful prayer. For Barth, the *Proslogion* represented the purest form of theological expression. But the converse is also true. Just as theology needs to become more prayerful, so prayer needs to become more theological. In ministering to God in the court of praise we need to use the rich resources of Scripture in order to worship God with our minds. We need to be as theological (certainly as Christological) as possible.

A third virtue in this kind of praise is that it is *practical*. By this I mean that it has consequences for evangelism. The discipline of using Christology in prayer functions like a branding iron, burning the ultimacy of Jesus into the thick hide of our lives. By constantly rehearsing the grounds of high Christology in prayer, we make our belief in the deity of Jesus one of the pillars of our spirituality. In the process we find that giving a defence for our hope in Jesus Christ (1 Peter 3.15) becomes more natural.

These, then, are just three of the main reasons why the prayer of high Christology is a virtuous, soul-affirming discipline. They show how important it is to go on from the gates of thanksgiving to the second stage in the Temple of God's presence. Here we spend time in the court of praise, praising God for his name. This is really what we might call 'the prayer of the mind'.

The prayer of the heart[6]

Having said all that I have to confess that there are days when I do not use this form of praise. There are days when I simply bow before God and say, like a little child, 'I love you. You are my Lord and my God. You are my Father and my Friend. I love you Lord'. This kind of praise I call 'the prayer of the heart'. It is a valid and invaluable form of praise. Indeed, God commands us to love him with all of our heart as well as with all our mind. Loving him with the whole of my mind is what the prayer of high Christology is about; but sometimes even this can feel inappropriate, and all that is needed on my part is a simple, 'I love you, Father'.

However, many of us will find this difficult. The ability to say 'I love you' to our Father in heaven will not come easily to those of us whose own childhood was not marked by physical affection and open declarations of love. This has been partly true for me. My family upbringing was not characterized by overt displays of love. The reason for that was because my own parents were themselves brought up on a model of family which was rooted in middle-class respectability and the repression of feelings. Consequently, in their parenting of me, my father and mother merely repeated a pattern which was almost certainly multi-generational.

But I recall a day some time ago when my father was staying not far from where I live. I felt a strong leading of the Spirit to go over to where he was and to tell him simply that I loved him. This was perhaps one of the hardest things I have ever done. I was terribly frightened of embarrassment or rejection. But when the moment came, my father put his arms around me, held me, and said 'I love you too'. It was an utterly transforming moment. From that time on, affection became natural. The years of tactile deprivation disappeared like a mist.

The prayer of the heart is prayer in which our feelings of love towards the Father are released from our fragile hearts. It is a simple 'I love you' to God. One such prayer from the heart can be worth a hundred prayers from the mind.

The prayer of the spirit

What goes for the heart also goes for the spirit. Sometimes it will seem good to us and to the Holy Spirit neither to pray with the mind nor even to pray from the heart like a child. Sometimes we are simply moved by the Holy Spirit into the language of the Spirit, the edifying and adorational use of the gift of tongues.

The charism of tongues, we should remember, is a ground-to-air phenomenon. It is prayer uttered by my spirit, prompted by the Holy Spirit, and directed heavenwards towards the throne. In this respect it differs from the gift of prophecy. Prophecy is an air-to-ground phenomenon. It is the revelation of the mind of Christ, through the Holy Spirit, to believers on the earth.

In the court of praise it is sometimes fitting and right to stand in awe of God and to be led by the Spirit into operating in this gift. Now obviously there are many Christians who do not speak in tongues. If you are one of those, please do not feel excluded by these words. Do not feel that your prayer life is any the less valid because of that. But at the same time, please appreciate the importance of tongues for others. One of its greatest virtues is that it helps people to overcome the problem of language which I mentioned at the start of this chapter. Praising God in tongues is the irrational language of an ecstatic spirit. It is worship that transcends words, and in that respect it is infinitely precious.

The prayer of the spirit is therefore a valid and edifying medium of praise.

Mind, Heart and Spirit

Of course in practice this division of mind, heart and spirit can prove to be artificial. At its best, praise involves all three dimensions of our being. To illustrate this, look at these words written by a busy housewife, after she had heard me speak not long ago about the gates of thanksgiving and the court of praise:

> In our bedroom I have a little table which I use as an altar. I lit my three candles and switched off all the lights and knelt, gazing up at the palm cross on the wall. The stillness and the candles helped me to remember that I'd come to thank and praise God and so I began. The amazing thing about thanksgiving is that you begin to realize just how many times God has blessed your life. You could spend hours on thanksgiving alone. I moved on into praise and decided to sing. I'd got a copy of *Mission Praise* and casually flipped over pages, looking for hymns of praise that I knew. Some of the ones I didn't know seemed to have such powerful words that I made up tunes as I went along. This became quite enjoyable and I must have spent twenty minutes or so picking out hymns which expressed how I felt. Then came the tongues. I like singing in tongues. Somehow, the sounds and 'words' remind me of the prayers chanted by the Jewish priests. It makes me feel special. No one knows what I am saying to God, it's so private and intimate. As I sang, new 'words' entered the language, which surprised me and one of them was the name 'Jesu'. I realized that my focus was changing and then slowly, gradually, there were just two sounds left, one of them being 'Jesu'. I found that an incredible feeling of peace was now surrounding me and I felt physically held, as though arms were supporting me and holding me still.

What a perfect example of the prayer of the mind (using the language of hymns), the prayer of the heart (song) and the prayer of the spirit (tongues)!

At its best, our prayers of praise will involve the body, the emotions, the spirit and the mind.

The Sacrifice of Praise

In conclusion, we do need to recognize that praising God requires sacrifice on our part. Perhaps that is why we are called to love God not only with all our minds, hearts and soul, but also with all our strength. Praise requires a strong sacrifice of the will in so far as we must *choose* to resist the call of the trivial and to obey the call to worship. The example from the letter just cited shows that an encounter with God must be preceded by a sacrifice of time and energy.

The court of praise, then, is about sacrifice. To remind us of this there is a large brazen altar in the centre of this inner court. This altar was known as the altar of sacrifice and was the place where the priests would perform any one of five sacrifices: the sin offering, the trespass offering, the burnt offering, the meal offering and the peace offering. We shall look at these in more detail in the next chapter. For the time being, just keep in mind that there is an altar of sacrifice in the court of praise. Keep in mind that praise is about giving, not receiving.

This truth needs to be emphasized in our day. So many people come to Church to get a blessing rather than to be a blessing. Even more of us depend upon our feelings when it comes to the degree of our involvement in worship itself. As such we are largely a generation which has lost the vision for sacrificial praise. At worst we are a culture of consumers who shop around for the church which best suits us, and then who only opt into those parts of a worship event which make us feel good.

Yet we are often reminded in Scripture of a different kind of 'consumerism'. Jesus said, 'zeal for your house will *consume* me' (John 2.17). In other words, 'my passion for your Temple will be the death of me; it will cost me everything'. This is a very far cry from today's religious consumerism. Instead of selfishness, this statement speaks of sacrifice. It shows us that true worship is not something which we consume, but rather something which consumes us. Jesus models a spirit of all-consuming self-denial in entering the court of praise. His words and actions remind us of the psalmist, who said 'We bring the sacrifice of praise into the house of the Lord' (Psalm 116.17).

As we begin our ministry of praise in the court of the priests, we can therefore do no better than to recall the exhortation, 'Through Jesus, therefore, let us continually offer up a sacrifice of praise –

the fruit of lips that confess his name' (Hebrews 13.15). As we do this, we shall prepare in the most meaningful and appropriate way for the sacrifice which we must make in the next stage of prayer, as we put our sins to death through the power of the Cross.

PRAYER

Almighty God, help me now, through Jesus, to offer up a sacrifice of praise. I want to confess Jesus in the court of praise. I want to celebrate the uniqueness of Jesus in a world that has reduced him to just a man. I want to praise Jesus for his uniqueness, his ultimacy and his deity.

Jesus, I praise you for the uniqueness of your name. I worship you because you are our Advocate in Heaven, the Bread of Life, the Consolation of Israel, the Door to Pastures New, Immanuel – God with us, the Friend of Sinners, our Great High Priest, the Holy One, Image of the Invisible God, Judge of All, King of Kings, Lord of Glory, Mighty God, the One and Only Son of Yahweh, the Prince of Peace and Righteous God, the Saviour of the World and our True Vine. I praise you for your character and confess you, Jesus, as the Messiah, the Son of the Living God.

Lord Jesus, with countless other kingdom priests, I praise you today in the inner court. I bring a sacrifice of praise into the house of the Lord. I confess your name with my lips, and I stand in awe of you. Amen.

3

THE ALTAR OF SACRIFICE

'Confession without change is just a game.'
Tom Harris, *I'm OK. You're OK*

In the year 740 BC, Isaiah entered the court of the priests in the Temple in Jerusalem. He made his way into the sanctuary, the holy place, and began his daily ministrations. Suddenly, the furniture and decor of the earthly Temple began to fade. In their place, new and heavenly counterparts began to emerge. In front of him, in what a few moments before had been the veiled entrance to the holy of holies, stood a great throne. On it, Isaiah saw Jehovah God, the Lord of all history and the Creator of the Universe. The long folds of his resplendent robes filled the sanctuary and flowed into the courts outside.

Above the throne strange, esoteric and celestial beings hovered motionlessly. They were on both sides of the throne, and were calling out the antiphons of heaven in deep melodious voices. 'Holy', they cried on one side; 'Holy' they replied on the other. As their sonorous voices gained in strength, Isaiah became aware of the ground shaking beneath his feet: the stronger the voices of the angels, the stronger the tremor of the stone around him. The great portals of the sanctuary began to shudder. The porch began to sway. Great clouds of smoke appeared from nowhere and Isaiah was filled with indescribable terror.

The prophet sank to his knees and then fell prostrate on the cold and trembling floor. His eyes filled with tears and, out of the deepest recesses of his soul, came a loud and tremulous cry: 'Woe is me. I am ruined. For I am a man of unclean lips and I live among a people of unclean lips, and my eyes have seen the King, the Lord Almighty!'

A few seconds passed. Then, as suddenly as it had begun, the shaking finished. The Temple stood still. Out of the corner of his eye Isaiah saw one of the seraphs above the throne fly to a great bronze altar and delicately lift a glowing ember from a small fragrant censor. Then the seraph flew towards Isaiah. The sound of its six wings as it hovered overhead seemed deafening in the silence. Isaiah looked up tentatively, and as he did so the seraph touched the prophet's lips with the coal. He felt no pain, no burning sensation upon his mouth or lips. A warm cleansing fire went straight down his throat and passed quickly through the whole of his body, and as it did so, the seraph pronounced absolution: 'Your guilt is taken away and your sin atoned for'.

With that, Isaiah stood up in the sanctuary of God's house. He was forgiven, he was cleansed, and he was ready to hear God.

The Importance of Confession

This story, recorded for us in Isaiah 6, reminds each one of us of the vital importance of confession in the Temple of prayer. As priests of the kingdom we need, as Isaiah did, to deal with the problem of our unholiness. We have entered God's gates with the ministry of gratitude. We have entered his courts with the ministry of praise. But before we go into the sanctuary we must pause and offer a ministry of sacrifice. This sacrifice is the sacrifice of true and heartfelt repentance (Psalm 51.17).

This is important because we can have no access to the holy place until we have confronted the *un*holy places in our own lives. At this third stage of prayer, we thus kneel before the great altar in the court of priests. Here we confess our sins to God. Here – if our repentance is sincere – we receive that same word of assurance that Isaiah received when his lips were touched by the burning coal: 'Your guilt is taken away. Your sins are atoned for'.

The Altar of Sacrifice

As we proceed through the gates of thanksgiving we are confronted in our imagination by a brass altar, elevated above the level of the court by about fifteen feet. We know that it was thirty feet long and was especially designed for various forms of sacrifice, but very little information is provided about this altar in Scripture. The writer of 2 Chronicles rather laconically remarks that 'Solomon made a bronze altar twenty cubits long, twenty cubits wide, and ten cubits high' (2 Chronicles 4.1). We do know that it was made of brass. Indeed, brass was the dominant metal in the court of the priests: the altar was brass, the great basin was brass, the small basins were made of brass, the two great pillars at the porch to the holy place were also brass. Since brass is symbolic of God's judgement in Scripture, we can see the significance of this. The court of the priests was decorated in brass because it was the place where sin was owned and dealt with.

The altar was the place of sacrifice. Five different sacrifices ordained by God and given to Moses were conducted here: the burnt offering (Leviticus 1), grain offering (Leviticus 2), peace offering (Leviticus 3), sin offering (Leviticus 4) and the guilt offering (Leviticus 5).

The burnt offering was made every morning and evening by the priests on behalf of the whole of Israel. The priest took a bull, or a sheep, or a bird – young, male and without defect – and slaughtered it. The blood was then taken from the dead animal and sprinkled against the altar. The animal's carcass was then stripped and burnt on the altar where it would produce 'an aroma pleasing to the Lord' (Leviticus 1.9).

The grain offering (the only bloodless offering) accompanied either the burnt, sin or peace offering. It consisted of grain or fine flour being burnt on the altar, along with olive oil, salt and incense. The Hebrew word for 'grain offering' can also be translated as 'gifts'. This highlights its purpose: the grain offering was a gift set aside for God which was to accompany one of three other offerings. It was a sign of the sinner's humble devotion.

The peace offering was made three times a year at the major Jewish festivals. The main purpose behind this sacrifice was obviously 'peace'. The Hebrew word for peace, '*shalom*', is often used of a peaceful or 'whole' relationship with God, with others, and with creation. The sacrifice itself consisted of the slaughter of an animal without defect. This could be offered on behalf of any of the many thousands of people who attended the three major Jewish festivals in the year.

The sin offering was a very specific sacrifice. It was designed for those who sinned unintentionally. If an anointed priest, or the whole of Israel, or a leader, or a member of the community of Israel committed sins in ignorance (i.e. not realizing at the time that they were sinning) then a sin offering was to be made by the priest as soon as the sin became known. Again, this involved the slaughter of a young animal.

The final offering was the guilt offering. This was traditionally known as 'the trespass offering' and was very similar to the sin offering. It was made in instances where restitution was feasible. In modern terms, if I stole a car from someone else, got caught and repented, the guilt offering would be made because I could return the car to the rightful owner. I would also find that I would have to pay a 20 per cent indemnity.

The Day of Atonement

More important than these sacrifices was the sacrifice occurring once each year on the Day of Atonement. This is described in Leviticus 16 and was performed by the high priest who took incense and blood from the brazen altar and went into the holy of holies (which only he was allowed to enter). Once behind the veil, the high priest arranged the burning, fragrant incense in a place where the smoke would cover the ark of the covenant. After that he took some of the blood and sprinkled it with his finger seven times over the front of the cover of the ark. Next he slaughtered a goat and took its blood behind the curtain, repeating the same procedure.

The high priest then came out of the sanctuary with blood from both the bull and the goat, and sprinkled it over the altar of sacrifice in the outer court. He took hold of a live goat, lay both hands upon the animal's head, and confessed over it the sins of the people of Israel. All their wickedness and rebellion was placed upon the head of the goat. The high priest then sent the goat out into the desert in the care of a man especially appointed for the task. The 'scapegoat' carried these sins to a solitary place, where the man released it.

Following that, the high priest bathed himself in the laver of water and put on his normal, priestly garments. He then went to the great brazen altar in the court of the priests to make a burnt offering for both himself and the Israelite nation. He also burnt the fat of the sin offering on this altar. Once this holy day was complete, then the people were released from their sins and clean in the sight of the Lord.

The Altar of the New Covenant

Before we turn to the practice of confession we need to remember that this ancient system of sacrifice has been rendered redundant by the atoning death of Jesus on the Cross. John's Gospel points out that Jesus is the Lamb of God who takes away the sin of the world (John 1.29, 36). Since lambs were slaughtered as a sin offering at Passover, this means that Calvary is the one perfect and final atonement for human sin. No more animals need to be slaughtered. No more offerings need to be burnt. Jesus has bridged the gap between humanity and God. Jesus has assumed our sin in his body on the Cross. He is Christ, the Passover Lamb, who has been sacrificed for us (compare 1 Corinthians 5.7). Thus the writer of the Hebrews declares:

> When Christ came as high priest of the good things that are already here, he went through the greater and more perfect tabernacle that is not man-made, that is to say, not a part of this creation. He did not enter by means of the blood of goats and calves; but he entered the Most Holy Place once and for all by his own blood, having obtained eternal redemption. The blood of goats and bulls and the ashes of a heiffer sprinkled on those who are ceremonially unclean sanctify them so that they are outwardly clean. *How much more, then, will the blood of Christ, who through the eternal Spirit offered himself unblemished to God, cleanse our consciences from acts that lead to death, so that we may serve the Living God!* (Hebrews 9.11–14).

In our ministry of sacrifice we therefore come to a new altar. The old altar has been supplemented: there is now a Cross in the court of praise. On this new altar of sacrifice we will find no other blood than that shed by Jesus, which cleanses us from all unrighteousness (Hebrews 13.10). This is the altar where we now must bow with humility.

The Nature of the Brazen Altar

There are four things which we need to understand about this altar as we approach the Cross for confession and repentance. First of all, we need to see it as a place of sincerity – a place where we resolve to deal with the sin in our lives in an honest way. As John wrote, 'If we say we have no sin we deceive ourselves' (1 John 1.8). So the first step is to resolve to be honest in owning and naming our sins. Secondly, we need to see the altar as a place of scrutiny – a place where we choose to examine our lives in the light of God's Word, in particular the Ten Commandments. Thirdly, we need to see this altar as a place of sacrifice – somewhere where we put sin to death. Fourthly, we must see it as a place of sanctification – a place where we are cleansed first of all through the blood of Christ, and secondly through the pure waters of the Holy Spirit.

A place of sincerity

The first thing to remember, then, is that the brazen altar is a place of sincerity. At this point I find it helpful to meditate on a comment, made by Tom Harris in his book *I'm OK. You're OK*: 'Confession without change is just a game'. In other words, mere apology is not enough. Saying sorry without the intention to stop sinning makes a mockery of confession. True confession always involves change: a change of mind, a change of heart, and a change of behaviour.

Say, for example, that I am presently struggling with the problem of bad language. If I am really serious about repenting, then I will be looking for three levels of transformation.

First of all, I will be looking for a change of mind. Having tolerated this habit, I now look upon it as a serious sin. I *name* this habit for what it is. I see from God's Word (e.g. Colossians 3.8) that filthy language is offensive to a holy God. I understand that it is contrary to God's Word and destructive to my relationships and to my Christian witness.

Secondly, I will be looking for a change of heart. Having become convinced that my behaviour is sinful, I now become convicted of having sinned. I get in touch with my feelings about using bad language. I feel guilty. I am sad that I have grieved the Holy Spirit. I may even weep at the realization of my sin. Like Isaiah I begin to recognize that I am literally a man of unclean lips, living among a people of unclean lips. In the process, I begin to feel differently. I no longer *want* to sin in this way. I experience a change of heart.

Thirdly, I will be looking for a change of behaviour. Having used a lot of foul language, I now co-operate with the Holy Spirit on a daily basis in what James calls 'the taming of the tongue' (James 3.1–12). I seek to work with the Lord in taking all my thoughts and words captive to the obedience of Jesus Christ. If I am very wise I might well ask another Christian – who sees me regularly and whom I trust – to observe my behaviour and to watch out for compromise. Now, at last, repentance is bearing observable fruit. I am experiencing a change of behaviour.

The altar of sacrifice is therefore a place of total sincerity. Nothing less than complete honesty will do in the presence of the Lord.

A place of scrutiny

The second thing to note about this altar is that it is a place of scrutiny. Here we need to remember the words of Lamentations 3.40: 'Let us examine our ways and test them, and let us return to the Lord'. How, then, do we examine or scrutinize our lives?

If we look again at the altar of sacrifice in the Temple we will notice that its measurements were all numerals of ten. The altar was ten cubits high, twenty cubits long, ten cubits wide. The number ten is the number of the Law in the Old Testament. When Moses received the relevation of God's Law on Mount Sinai he received it in the form of the Ten Commandments. This points to the abiding significance of the commandments in relation to holiness. If we want to enter the holy place of God's presence, then we need to scrutinize our lives and make sure that we have not broken any of the Ten Commandments. As John wrote, 'Everyone who sins breaks the Law; in fact, sin is lawlessness' (1 John 3.4).

The Ten Commandments are known as the Decalogue, after the Greek words '*deca*' (meaning ten) and '*logos*' (meaning command). They are summarized in Exodus 20 and Deuteronomy 5:

1 No other gods
2 No idolatry
3 No blasphemy
4 No abuse of the Sabbath
5 No disrespect for parents
6 No murder
7 No adultery
8 No stealing
9 No false testimony
10 No covetousness.

These ten commands represent God's 'no-go' areas for his people. They are boundaries which were designed to protect us, not to punish us. If we keep within these boundaries, if we observe these laws, we shall live under the blessing of God. If we depart from them, then God's blessing will depart from us too.

A world of lawlessness

It is fair to say that the societies of Western Europe now virtually ignore the Ten Commandments. Countries in the West were, for hundreds of years, constructed around the Law of Moses. Their legal systems were based on it. Their stability depended upon it. However, the Age of Enlightenment produced a widespread secularism in which God was increasingly pushed to the sidelines. As a result, societies became increasingly post-Christian and, in the process, the commandments given to Moses became an ancient and dusty irrelevance.

In Great Britain, all Ten Commandments are openly ignored or flouted today. As British culture and society become increasingly alienated from God, people turn to idols such as money, status, success and sex as surrogate objects of worship or 'gods'. Everywhere, the names of God and of Jesus are taken in vain. There is no respect for Sunday as a holy day; it is now a day of trading like any other. The family unit is decaying rapidly; young people rebel against their parents – if they have parents. Murder is rife, even of babies, toddlers and the elderly. The sanctity of marriage has been forgotten; divorce costs Britain £4 million a day and adultery is on the increase. Stealing is widespread – from the secreting of unaccounted stationery to the taking and wrecking of other peoples' cars. With the breakdown of community, neighbours now fight and litigate over parking spaces and garden fences. Finally, in a culture designated as the 'me' generation, many regard the property of others as fair game.

The problem of idolatry

Infringements of all the commandments are widespread today but the one which is broken most flagrantly is the second, the prohibition against idolatry:

> 'You shall not make for yourself an idol in the form of anything in heaven above or in the waters below. You shall not bow down to them or worship them; for I, the Lord your God, am a jealous God, punishing the children for the sin of the fathers to the third and fourth generation of those who hate me, but showing love to a thousand of those who love me and keep my commandments' (Deuteronomy 5.8–10).

In Moses' day, idolatry was easy to spot. If a group of Israelites melted a precious metal, formed it into a large animal, then started bowing down to it and worshipping it, you could be fairly sure that they were suffering from a severe case of idolatry. It would not take the mind of a great saint to diagnose this condition. Idolatry was a *visible* phenomenon. Today, however, idolatry is more difficult to define because it is more invisible. We do not see people prostrate before large metal sculptures in our high streets or backyards. What we *do* see is people emotionally dependent upon various objects, substances, goals and relationships. We see people who are suffering from an idolatry which does not consist of an overt devotion to a manmade idol but rather of a disguised obsession of the heart. Anything which, to use Luke Johnson's words, 'rivets my attention, centres my activity, preoccupies my mind, and motivates my action', is my god or my idol. As Johnson concludes,

'That in virtue of which I act is god; that for which I will give up anything else is my god'.[1]

Money, sex and power

What, then, are the attachments or idols which are most prevalent today? The fact is there are so many that it would be impossible to provide an exhaustive list of them. People seem to be dependent upon a great variety of things. I have seen clear examples of idolatrous attachment to food, shopping, clothes, home-making, DIY, sport, fitness, money, status, home technology, sex, relation-ships, ideologies, alcohol, prescription drugs, illicit drugs, choc-olate, and so on. But the three idols which seem to grip and destroy people more than any other are, as Richard Foster has rightly shown, the idols of money, sex and power.[2]

In 1 John 2.15–17, the apostle commands us not to love the world. He identifies three idols which are particularly dangerous: the lust of the flesh; the lust of the eyes; the pride of life. The lust of the flesh can be defined as the unbridled drive to express one's passion – specifically sexual passion. The lust of the eyes can be defined as the unbridled drive to amass our possessions – specifi-cally material possessions. The pride of life can be defined as the unbridled drive to establish our position in life – specifically a position of status and dominance over others. These three drives, once activated, force a person on to a slippery slope of destructive lifestyle which I am describing as 'idolatry'. They are drives which encourage the worship of money, sex and power.

The power of these drives means that we, as Christians, must learn to be ruthless with any sign of idolatry in our own lives. We have to confront our idols through a process of self-scrutiny. That is why the apostle John ends his first letter with the words: 'Dear children, keep yourselves from idols'. John is urging us constantly to watch our own lives and make sure that we are not starting to become preoccupied with someone or something other than God. God will bless us in our sexuality, in our material needs and in our position in life just so long as they are all under his Lordship.

A place of sacrifice

Honest scrutiny must be followed by ruthless sacrifice. Sacrifice is a vivid metaphor for the confession of sin. The altar of sacrifice was, after all, a place of execution. In the era of the old covenant, animals were brutally killed on this altar. In the era of the new covenant, Jesus was also brutally killed. He was flogged so hard that the flesh and muscle on his back was torn to shreds. A crown of thorns was rammed on to his head, puncturing his scalp. He was forced to carry a heavy cross-beam to a rubbish dump outside Jerusalem, where long iron spikes were hammered through the median nerve in his wrists and feet. He was then hauled up on the cross where every movement would have been agony. The altar of sacrifice is therefore not a safe, hygienic place, neither in the Old nor in the New Testament. This altar has a suggestion of brutality about it. It is a place of finality, not a place of frivolity.

When Paul talks about dealing with sin he uses the violent language of sacrifice and of execution. In Colossians 3.5 he writes, 'Put to death, therefore, whatever belongs to your earthly nature'. The vocabulary here is extremely important. Notice that Paul does not say, 'Apologize to God'. Paul says 'Put sin to death'. The word translated 'put to death' is *nekrosate*, an imperative form of the verb *nekroo*. In the noun form the word is *nekrosis*, the word used by Paul in 2 Corinthians 4.10 where he writes, 'We always carry about in our body the putting to death (*nekrosis*) of Jesus'. Since the manner of Jesus' death was crucifixion, we can confirm that Paul is speaking in violent terms in Colossians 3.5. In relation to our personal holiness, Paul is saying 'Be ruthless with the things of the earthly nature. Put them to death!'

The practice of sacrifice

Most of us have few problems putting an occasional sin to death, one that is, as it were, 'out of character' and rare. Where problems arise is in the termination of habitual sins, of addictive patterns of sinful behaviour. How do we deal with this kind of sin with finality?

I believe we have a great deal to learn about finishing abitual sin from those who help addicts – Alcoholics Anonymous (AA) and related groups. These bodies have a programme for dealing with addiction. I have adapted these steps so as to make them relevant for Christians who want to confess some area of their lives where habitual sin or addictive habits have taken control:

Step 1   I admit that I am powerless over my addiction – that my life has become unmanageable.

Step 2   I confess that the Holy Spirit, God's power, can restore me to wholeness.

Step 3   I make a decision to turn my will and my life over to the care of the living God.

Step 4   I make a searching and fearless moral inventory of myself.

Step 5   I admit to God, to myself, and to another trusted Christian friend the exact nature of my sins.

Step 6   I make myself ready to let God remove all my defects.

Step 7   I humbly ask the Lord to remove my shortcomings. In the company of trusted friends I renounce idolatry and pray for deliverance.

Step 8   I make a list of all persons I have harmed, and I become willing to make amends to them all.

Step 9   I make direct amends to such people wherever possible, except when to do so would injure them or others.

Step 10   I continue to make a personal inventory and when I go wrong, I promptly admit it.

Step 11   I seek through prayer to improve my relationship with God, praying for more love and more power to live a holy and a healed life.

Step 12   Having had a spiritual awakening as the result of these steps, I try to carry this message to others.

Learning from AA

There are a number of things we can learn about ruthless confession from this twelve-step programme. First and foremost, we learn the value of community. Christians have a highly individualistic conception of repentance: we think that we can destroy our idols all on our own. The AA and related groups, on the other hand, have a different philosophy. They know that freedom is only possible through community. Addicts need the help of others if they are to be liberated – others who will challenge, comfort and assist them. A supporting network of relationships is therefore essential. As James puts it, 'Confess your sins to one another and you will be healed' (James 5.16).

Secondly, we have a lot to learn from the ninth step, in which the addict is encouraged to go and apologize to all those who have been harmed by his behaviour. This again is pertinent to confession. The AA programme reminds us of the old Christian truth that the circle of confession should be related to the circle of commission. If I have committed a sin against God, I confess to God. If I have committed a sin against someone else, I confess to them. If I have committed a sin against the Church, I confess to the Church, and so on.

Thirdly, we have a lot to learn from the realism of this programme. Addicts know that they will be tempted to fall again. They are therefore not complacent. They keep on subjecting their lives to a fearless moral inventory. This too is relevant. Although we make every effort to repent truly, we recognize our weakness as human beings and that we may be tempted in similar areas again. We therefore take steps to ensure that we do not knowingly enter contexts of temptation, areas of life where we will be vulnerable to falling again.

A place of sanctification

The altar is therefore a place of sacrifice and this of course means that we have a part to play in the matter of personal sanctification – the process by which we become more holy. We have to be sincere. We have to scrutinize our lives. We have to own, name and terminate our sins with the help of the Holy Spirit.

This needs emphasizing in our day. Most people forget their own part in this process. In my experience, people often have one of two understandings of sanctification. These two views we might call a *feminine* and a *masculine* view. If some psychologists are right when they say that masculinity is about 'initiating' and femininity is about 'receiving', then the masculine view of sanctification is this: 'I become holy by striving to do what the Bible tells me to do'.

The feminine view of sanctification is the opposite: this view says, 'It is not for me to take the initiative. Sanctification is a matter of me receiving more and more of God's Holy Spirit. All I need to do is to keep open. God will do the rest'.

Both of these perspectives are half true. There is a masculine aspect to sanctification. When Paul says, 'Put sin to death', he is addressing Christians in the church at Colossae. They, not God, are the subject of the imperative, *nekrosate*. It is they who must work and strive towards holiness. Indeed we see this everywhere in Paul's writings. It is we who must take the initiative in the battle against the flesh. We are to be the executioners of sin. But there is undoubtedly a feminine aspect as well. Not only are we to fight, to wrestle, to struggle and to strive; we are also to remember that we are not alone in the battle. The Holy Spirit is at work within us to restore the image of Jesus Christ in our lives. That is why Paul encourages us to put to death the deeds of the body by the power of the Spirit (Romans 8.13). The command to terminate sin (*thanatoute*, literally 'mortify') is accompanied by the assurance that the Holy Spirit will assist us in this task. We are not alone!

So when Paul says, 'Put sin to death' he is showing that we have personal responsibility for dealing with sin. We are accountable to God in the area of holiness. But, at the same time, God does not leave us to wage the war against our flesh on our own. If we co-operate with his Holy Spirit then the war will be won a great deal more easily. We need to 'go on being filled with the Holy Spirit' (Ephesians 5.18) if we are to be sanctified.

The promise of cleansing

John wrote, 'If we confess our sins, God is faithful and just and will forgive us our sins and *cleanse* us from all unrighteousness' (1 John 1.9). These words contain a condition and a promise. The condition is that we must confess our sins, in other words admit before the judgement seat of God that we have wandered from God's ways. As we do that, Jesus our Advocate pleads on our behalf (1 John 2.1) and the Father forgives us. That is the promise. He will be faithful and just; that is, true to his Word. He will both pardon and cleanse us.

As we confess our sins, Jesus therefore starts the process of cleansing us. Just as Jesus drove out the money-changers and the pigeon-fanciers in the Temple in Jerusalem, so Jesus drives out the sin and idolatry in our bodies. Just as Jesus cleansed the Temple in Jerusalem in the yesterday of history, so he cleanses the temple of my body in the today of my discipleship, and in the tomorrow of my walk with him. Jesus is the same yesterday, today and forever (Hebrews 13.8). What he did in the Temple nearly 2,000 years ago he will go on doing in the temples of our bodies and in the new temple of his Church.

The molten sea

As if to remind us of this promise of cleansing, there is not only an altar in the court of praise. There is also a molten sea – a huge bronze basin which rested on twelve bronze oxen (2 Chronicles 4.2–6, 15; 1 Kings 7.23–6, 44; 1 Chronicles 18.8). This contained water for the purification of the priests (2 Chronicles 4.6).

If the brazen altar is a place of making sacrifice, the molten sea is a place of receiving cleansing; if the one is a place of blood, the other is a place of water. This should remind us of Calvary, for on the Cross there flowed both blood and water from the side of the Saviour (John 19.34). As the old revival hymn puts it:

> On the Mount of Crucifixion
> Fountains opened deep and wide;
> Through the floodgates of God's mercy
> Flowed a vast and gracious tide.
> Grace and love, like mighty rivers,
> Poured incessant from above,
> And heaven's peace and perfect justice
> Kissed a guilty world in love.

We should never forget that the pardon and purity which we receive at the altar of sacrifice are gifts of Calvary.

The Art of Confession

So the third stage of prayer in the Temple of God's presence requires that we should spend time before the altar of sacrifice – a place of sincerity, of scrutiny, of sacrifice and of sanctification. Having looked backwards in thanksgiving (stage 1), and upwards in praise (stage 2), we now look inwards in confession (stage 3).

Kneeling before the altar of sacrifice, we therefore need to cultivate the ability to look inwards in a healthy way. In doing this we must beware of two extremes: toxic self-denigration on the one hand, and blind self-righteousness on the other. Self-righteousness is a particular danger. That is why Jesus told this parable:

> Two men went up to the Temple to pray, one a Pharisee and the other a tax collector. The Pharisee stood up and prayed about himself: 'God, I thank you that I am not like other men – robbers, evildoers, adulterers – or even like this tax collector. I fast twice a week and give a tenth of all I get'. But the tax collector stood at a distance. He would not even look up to heaven, but beat his breast and said, 'God, have mercy on me, a sinner' (Luke 18.9–14).

We must be careful not to indulge in Pharisaical fantasies about our level of righteousness. The Pharisee was guilty precisely of this. But at the same time we must also be careful not to be tempted into diseased self-hatred. Self-righteousness and self-hatred are both forms of self-indulgence. They are altogether too influenced by our own view of ourselves, rather than by God's view of us. The example of the publican shows that it is possible to grieve about our inner state without feeling rejected by God. Jesus said of this man that he, not the Pharisee, went home justified before God. In other words, he went home knowing that he had been, in the words of the hymn, 'ransomed, healed, restored, forgiven'.

The practice of confession

Spontaneous confession (Psalm 51)
Sometimes the actual practice of confession involves a simple cry

of the heart. Like the tax collector we weap before God and cry, 'God, have mercy on me, a sinner'.

Scriptural confession
At other times, it might be more appropriate to engage in a meditation on the Ten Commandments. This might involve thinking carefully about each commandment, and then allowing the Spirit to illuminate areas of sin in ourselves and in our society. Something like this may sometimes be more fitting:

1   *You shall have no other gods but me*
   Lord, I acknowledge you as the One True Living God, revealed in Jesus of Nazareth. Keep me pure in my devotion to you. Help me not to be deceived by the voices around me into thinking that there are other gods beside you. Help me to make a firm stand in this pluralistic culture and to say, 'There is one God, the God and Father of our Lord Jesus Christ'. Help me to love you with all of my heart, all of my soul, all of my mind, and all of my strength today and every day.

2   *You shall not make for yourself any idol*
   Lord, help me not to be over-dependent upon anyone or anything other than you. You are an All-Sufficient God. I do not need money, sex or power to be a fulfilled person. Today I renounce money, sex, power and all their works in my life. I ask you to help me to be obedient to the ethical requirements of the kingdom. Help me to live a lifestyle of detachment, not attachment. Help me to be addicted to Jesus alone.

3   *You shall not dishonour the name of the Lord your God*
   Lord, keep me from ever taking your name – or the name of your Son – in vain. Help me to be bold and firm when others do so. Help me to warn them of their sin. Today I renounce blasphemy and all foul language. I take every thought and word of mine captive to the obedience of Jesus Christ and I ask that you would give me clean lips in this generation of unclean lips. I put this sin to death on the altar.

4   *Remember the Lord's Day and keep it holy*
Lord, forgive me that Sunday is not always the highlight of my
week. Forgive me that so often I endure it and spoil it. Help me
to rejoice and be glad in this day that you have made. Help
me to set it apart from all other days. Help me to take a stand
against Sunday trading and to draw my friends and family back
to a biblical use of this day. Lord, make Sunday special again in
this nation. Make it a truly Christ-centred day.

5   *Honour your father and your mother*
Lord, I think of where I am today in my relationship with my
parents. I recall that dishonouring thoughts, words and actions
are detrimental to my walk with you. Help me to honour,
revere and obey my parents – even in the trivial tasks of tele-
phoning or letter-writing. And Lord, forgive our nation for
breaking this commandment on such a massive scale. Heal
dysfunctional families. Restore biblical values in the home.

6   *You shall not murder*
Lord, forgive our society for breaking this sixth commandment. There are reports of horrible murders every day. The
most vulnerable people – babies, toddlers and the elderly – are
often the targets. What has become of us? Lord, we cry to you
to have mercy upon us. Have mercy upon me, too. I remember
that Jesus said that to have a violent thought about someone
was to commit murder in your eyes. Forgive me for the aggres-
sive fantasies I have had about those who have hurt me. Help
me to forgive and to be reconciled.

7   *You shall not commit adultery*
Lord, I remember today that you created marriage and that
you invented sex. I therefore submit to your Word in these
matters. Help me to remember your abhorrence of *porneia* – of
sexual intercourse outside of marriage. I reflect again on your
call to sexual holiness in 1 Thessalonians 4.3–8 and say, 'Lord,
forgive me for all trace of sexual immorality'. I conduct a
fearless moral inventory of my sexuality right now and I put to
death on the altar all those thoughts, words and actions which
are contrary to your Word. I ask you to forgive me.

8   *You shall not steal*

Lord, help me not to be wordly in this area. Forgive me that I so often lack complete integrity in the matter of stationery, expenses, bills and taxes. Help me to see even misdemeanours as infringements of this eighth commandment. Help me to see them as serious sin. Please forgive me for my worldliness. Help me to be different by putting to death all compromise in this area.

9   *You shall not be a false witness*

Lord, I ask you to forgive me for the things that I have said against others – cynical, destructive, evil things. Help me to live in love and peace with all people. Help me not to slander and criticize in order to be popular or accepted. Forgive me that my relationships with those who are literally my neighbours is not all that it could be. Lord have mercy upon me. I put to death the habit of false testimony. I choose instead to speak the truth in love.

10 *You shall not covet*

Lord, I admit that I sometimes look at someone else's house, someone else's salary, someone else's lifestyle, someone else's spouse, and I wish that I had what they had. I put the sin of covteousness to death and I choose to celebrate with a dance of gratitude that which you have, so graciously, given to me.

Liturgical confession

Also helpful is the use of set prayers of confession, especially when there is no obvious sense of sin in our lives. I often use an adapted and personalized version of the prayer of confession in the Anglican liturgy:

> Almighty God, my Heavenly Father,
> I confess that I have sinned against you
> and against others,
> in thought, word and deed,
> through negligence, through weakness,
> through my own deliberate fault.

> For the sake of your Son Jesus Christ,
> who died for me,
> please forgive me for all that is past,
> and grant that I may serve you
> in newness of life,
> to the glory of your holy name,
> Amen.

It is also helpful to use the following prayer of confession, known as the *widduy*, which forms the heart of the Jewish Yom Kippur. The section I am about to cite is called the *al het* and is again an adapted, personalized version:[3]

> May it be your will, O Lord our God and God of our fathers, to forgive me for all my sins, to pardon me for all my iniquities, and to grant me remission for my transgressions.

> For the sin which I have committed before you under compulsion, or of my own will . . .

> For the sin which I have committed before you through the hardening of my heart . . .

> For the sin which I have committed before you out of ignorance . . .

> For the sin which I have committed before you through the utterances of my lips . . .

> For the sin which I have committed before you by unchastity . . .

> For the sin which I have committed before you openly and secretly . . .

> For all these, O God of forgiveness, forgive me, pardon me, grant me remission . . .

> Through Jesus Christ, who died for me. Amen.

Whichever form of confessional prayer one uses, the important thing is to come to the brazen altar prepared for sincerity, scrutiny, sacrifice and sanctification.

Divine amnesia

Above all, it is important to come to the altar with trust in God. God promises in his word: 'I will forgive their wickedness and will remember their sins no more' (Jeremiah 31.34).

Here we are confronted with the ineffable grace of God. God says, 'I will completely forget the sins which you confess'. This means that when I truly repent of sin in my life, from that moment on God suffers from a permanent and complete forgetfulness concerning that sin! I call this forgetfulness, 'divine amnesia'. Divine amnesia comes into operation when we pray to God, saying 'I've done it again, Lord'. If we truly repented the first time, God will reply, 'Done what again?'

So, come to the altar trusting in God's promises. God is omnipotent, yes. But there is one thing he will not and cannot do, and that is lie. So if God promises it, that should settle it. He will keep his word. He will remember our sins no more.

PRAYER

Lord, I confess all my sins before you now. I put them all to death on the Cross, the new altar of sacrifice. I ask for your Holy Spirit to help me to terminate all unholy things in my life. And I ask you to help me to change, not just in my thoughts and in my feelings, but also in my behaviour. Lord have mercy upon me. Pardon me through the blood of Christ and cleanse me in the water of your Spirit. Thank you, Jesus, for the blood and the water in the court of praise. Thank you for dying for me. Amen.

4

THE HOLY PLACE

O Thou, who camest from above
The pure celestial fire to impart,
Kindle a flame of sacred love
On the mean altar of my heart.

Charles Wesley

Further Up and Further In

We have now entered God's gates with thanksgiving, entered the inner court with praise, and confessed our sins at the altar of sacrifice. Having received God's pardon and cleansing, we now climb the steps to the sanctuary, a great building known as the holy place. Before us are two bronze pillars which stand before the huge portals to the sanctuary. This is the last time we shall see anything made of bronze as we pray in the Temple of the Lord's presence. Everything from now on will be made of gold rather than bronze. The bronze of judgement is now replaced by the gold of majesty.

All this shows how our ministry as kingdom priests is, in reality, a journey into God. The subtitle of this book is called 'Deeper into God in prayer'. That is because I see the different stages of prayer as a gradual pilgrimage in which we go 'further up and further in' to the heart of God. The change from bronze to gold signifies the progress of this journey. The need to climb steps up to the sanctuary has the same effect. All the time we are obeying the call in James 4.8: 'Come near to God and he will come near to you'.

The Table of Shewbread

At this stage of the journey, I like to imagine Jesus, our Great High Priest, leading me through the great doorway of the sanctuary, into the hall, and then onwards to various parts of the holy place, all of which have a significance in the ministry of prayer.

The first place where we pause to pray is at the golden table of shewbread. This table was carefully tended by the priests. Thus we read in 1 Chronicles that

> The duty of the Levites was to help Aaron's descendants in the service of the Temple of the Lord: to be in charge of the courtyards, the side rooms, the purification of all sacred things and the performance of other duties at the house of God. They were in charge of the bread set out on the table, the flour for the grain offerings, the unleavened wafers, the baking and the mixing, and all measurements of quantity and size (23.28–9).

This table was made of wood but was overlaid with gold. It was two feet high, three feet long and about eighteen inches wide. On the top of the table were twelve pieces of unleavened shewbread. These were in two piles of six pieces. Every week, on the Sabbath, the priests replenished the shewbread. The old bread was theirs to eat. The new bread was to remain in the holy place until the following Sabbath.

The symbolism of the shewbread is this: the twelve pieces of bread represent the twelve tribes of Israel; the bread itself represents God's gracious provision of bread from heaven ('manna') when the Israelites were hungry in the desert. The golden table of shewbread therefore reminds us of the importance of petitionary prayer, of praying for our own, personal needs. It reminds us of the petition in the disciple's prayer, 'Give us this day our daily bread'.

So our first duty in the holy place is to petition for our own needs. Jesus himself encouraged us to petition when he said, 'Ask, and it will be given to you; seek, and you will find; knock, and the door will be opened to you' (Matthew 7.7). Jesus was legitimating the practice of self-orientated prayer. He was actually encouraging us to spend time praying for ourselves. He was telling us to

A – sk
S – eek
K – nock.

The Problem of Petition

Many people have real difficulties with this kind of prayer. Most of these problems stem from a genuine sense of triviality; in other words, from the feeling that our needs are too small for God's attention. Consequently, many people never pray for the little things for the same reason that they do not come to me in the parish. They decide not to call because they honestly feel that their need is too small and that my time is too limited.

But God the Father is not an exhausted vicar who has little time for the trivial. He is a Father who has the same amount of time for everyone and for everything. That is because in heaven there is no time. The Father is addressing our needs from a point beyond time and space. He can therefore be meeting my need in Grenoside at the same time as he is meeting the needs of others in Grenoble. God is not confined as we are. We can therefore approach him with confidence.

Give Us This Day Our Daily Bread

Notice that it is our most basic needs that God is interested in hearing about. That is why it is so important that we see the significance of the word 'bread' in the petition, 'Give us this day our daily *bread*'. There could hardly be anything more mundane than bread – there are few things which we take more for granted! Yet it is daily bread that Jesus says we should pray for. Not luxury holidays, not huge salaries, not expensive meals, but *bread*.

There is therefore plenty of justification for coming to the golden table and for asking the Lord to meet our needs. This is not a place where we demand luxuries. It is a place where we ask for 'the bare necessities of life'. That is why Jesus says in Matthew 7.9–11:

85

> Which of you, if his son asks for bread, will give him a stone? Or if he asks for a fish, will give him a snake? If you, then, though you are evil, know how to give good gifts to your children, *how much more will your Father in heaven give good gifts to those who ask him*!

God longs to hear us asking for good gifts; that is gifts that are good in the sight of God, and good for us. God longs to give us those things which will help us to live in harmony with his will.

The Abuse of Petition

This last point is extremely important: God longs to give us those things which will help us to live in harmony with his will. In other words, he promises those things which are consistent both with his character and with his purposes.

This truth requires emphasis in our times. Today there is a growing body of Christians all over the world who are employing some of the values of prosperity Christianity in the practice of petition. Many are taking the words of Jesus in John 14.14 at face value: 'You may ask me for *anything* in my name and I will give it to you'. These words are used by prosperity teachers to suggest that we have access to the 'blessings' of health and wealth. All we have to do is 'name it and claim it'. Did not Jesus say 'ask for *anything*?' 'Well then', say the prosperity teachers. 'Ask for whatever you want and just believe for it!'

This kind of teaching is extremely dangerous. The problem with it is that it does not take into consideration what Jesus meant by 'asking in his name'. In the Palestinian culture of Jesus' day, a person's name summed up their whole personality. Their name was symbolic of their character. When Jesus said, 'You may ask me for anything in my name', he was therefore saying, 'You may ask me for the kinds of things which I myself would ask for'. Since it is inconceivable to think of Jesus ever asking for financial prosperity for his own sake, there can be no grounds for self-indulgence in petitionary prayer. Indeed, we should heed the warning given by James, the brother of the Lord Jesus: 'When you ask, you do not receive, because you ask with wrong motives, that you may spend what you get on your pleasures' (James 4.3).

The Practice of Petition

Having said that, we should not lose sight of the fact that the Father desires to give good gifts to those who ask. Good gifts, in my view, are those gifts which enable us to function more effectively as disciples of the Lord Jesus. As the apostle John wrote, 'This is the confidence we have in approaching God: that if we ask anything according to his will, he hears us. And if we know that he hears us – whatever we ask – we know that we have what we asked of him' (1 John 5.14–15).

So if physical pain or illness is preventing us from working for the kingdom, it is not wrong to go to the Father and ask for relief from distress, for healing from illness. What father would refuse to comfort his child if that child was in pain, or needed a bandage? So it is with God. While there are times when illness can be a form of vocation, there are also many times when it is not, when it is right to ask the Father for healing.

The same goes not only for physical but also for material needs. If lack of money is causing us to focus more on essential needs than the business of the kingdom, we should ask the Father for help in meeting our needs. I can remember many an occasion when I had to go to my father when I got into trouble financially at university. He was always willing to set me back on my feet again, though he was not always able to! How much more will our Heavenly Father be concerned that we should not worry about our lives, about what we will eat, drink, wear (Matthew 6.25–34). How proper it is, therefore, to take our essential material needs to God in prayer, and then to trust him to provide what is right for us.

The same goes for other needs, in particular those relating to our emotions. If anxiety or depression is weighing us down and debilitating us in our work for the Lord, then it is here – at the golden table of shewbread – that we should cast our anxiety upon the Lord, knowing that he cares for us (1 Peter 5.7). It is here that we should plead with him for comfort, help, clarity, direction, wholeness. Whatever the nature of our dark night of the soul, God will want to walk there with us and guide us to the dawn of a new day.

The Golden Lampstands

If the Father is concerned about our physical, material and emotional needs, he is also concerned about all our other needs. He is particularly concerned to meet our spiritual needs. Here I find the golden lampstands a useful symbol and memory aid. The golden lampstands remind me of the spiritual resources which God graciously provides for his children.

One of the duties of the priests in the Temple was to rekindle the lampstands. There were ten of these in the holy place, five on each side of the chamber (1 Kings 7.49). Each of these was fashioned according to the instructions in Exodus 25.31–40:

> Make a lampstand of pure gold and hammer it out, base and shaft; its flower-like cups, buds and blossoms shall be of one piece with it. Six branches are to extend from the sides of the lampstand – three on one side and three on the other. . . . The buds and branches shall all be of one piece with the golden lampstand, hammered out of pure gold. Then make it seven lamps and set them up on it so that they light the space in front of it. Its wick trimmers and trays are to be of pure gold. A talent of pure gold is to be used for the lampstand and all these accessories. See that you make them according to the pattern shown you on the mountain.

The seven-branched lampstands, also known as the *menorah*, were an impressive feature of the holy place.

The Good Gifts of the Spirit

From the time of the early church, the *menorah* has been seen as a symbol of the so-called sevenfold gifts of the Spirit.[1] The basis for this is the prophecy concerning the Messiah in Isaiah 11.2–3a:

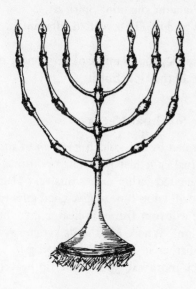

The Spirit of Yahweh will rest on him –
  the spirit of wisdom and of understanding,
  the spirit of counsel and of might,
  the spirit of the knowledge and fear of Yahweh,
and he will delight in the fear of Yahweh.

The central shaft of the *menorah* was understood to symbolize the Holy Spirit. The other three pairs of branches were understood to symbolize different manifestations or gifts of the Holy Spirit. The first pair, wisdom and understanding, were seen as manifestations of the mind or the intellect. The second pair, counsel and might, were seen to relate to planning and strength. The third pair, the knowledge and the fear of Yahweh, were seen as gifts to help us in our relationship with God.

This symbolism lies behind the words of the ancient hymn, which begins:

> Come, Holy Ghost, our souls inspire,
> And lighten with celestial fire.

> Thou the anointing Spirit art,
> Who dost Thy sevenfold gifts impart.

This hymn is itself a good example of petitionary prayer, of asking for the good gifts of the Holy Spirit.

Petitioning for Spiritual Needs

So we are reminded by the golden *menorah* of the importance of asking for spiritual, not just physical, resources. Luke's version of Jesus' promise cited earlier makes this very plain: 'If you, then, though you are evil, know how to give good gifts to your children, how much more will your Father in heaven give the Holy Spirit to those who ask him!' Where Matthew's version reads, 'how much more will your Father in heaven give good gifts', Luke's version reads, 'how much more will your Father in heaven give the Holy Spirit!'

There are many spiritual gifts which we can ask for. The following is a list of the ones I have noticed, and they are certainly greater in number than just seven.

Pronouncement gifts
These are gifts which involve pronouncing the mind of God to a congregation.

1 *Prophecy* (Romans 12.6, 1 Corinthians 12.10) An anointing in which a person is enabled to communicate God's will to a church through a vision, dream, picture, Scripture, message or impression. It often involves a predictive dimension.
2 *Teaching* (Romans 12.7, Ephesians 4.11, 1 Corinthians 12.28) An anointing in which a person is enabled to expound and apply the Word of God in such a way that the listener is impacted by a sense of revelation, and then encouraged to a personal transformation.

People gifts

These are gifts which God gives to help us in our relationships with both believers and unbelievers.

3   *Encouragement* (Romans 12.8)   An anointing in which a person is led to say or write something which builds up a fellow Christian in the faith.

4   *Evangelism* (Ephesians 4.11)   While all are called to share the Gospel, some are given a special endowment or ability in this work. This is the gift of evangelism: an anointing in which a person is given the power to know with whom the Gospel should be shared, when it should be shared, and how.

5   *Hospitality* (1 Peter 4.9)   An anointing in which a person is enabled to open his or her home to others. It is also an anointing in which Christians are enabled to invite and welcome outsiders into a church fellowship.

6   *Apostleship* (1 Corinthians 12.28, Ephesians 4.11)   An anointing in which God empowers a person to go out from a church-base to establish a new church somewhere else.

7   *Leadership* (Romans 12.8, 1 Thessalonians 5.12)   An anointing in which a person is given the ability to lead people in such a way that they want to follow.

8   *Mercy* (Romans 12.8)   An anointing in which a person is moved by divine compassion to acquire and to give aid to the poor, the suffering and the oppressed.

9   *Pastoral care* (Ephesians 4.11)   An anointing in which God gives a person a heart to shepherd or look after a body of believers with great sensitivity and with practical care.

Practical gifts

These are gifts which involve less visible but equally valuable labour in the kingdom.

10   *Administration* (1 Corinthians 12.28)   An anointing in which a person is enabled to draw up and maintain rotas, to make plans, to keep accounts, and the like.

11   *Craftsmanship* (Exodus 31.3–6)   An anointing in which a person is enabled to use artistic gifts for the Church (e.g.

composing songs, playing musical instruments, creating banners, drawing pictures, writing poetry).

12   *Giving* (Romans 12.9)   An anointing in which someone is especially motivated to give of self, time and/or money for the work of the Church.

13   *Helping* (1 Corinthians 12.28)   An anointing in which someone is especially enabled to give practical help, such as setting up rooms, clearing up chairs.

Power gifts

These are gifts which are more obviously the product of the supernatural power of the Holy Spirit.

14   *Knowledge* (1 Corinthians 12.8)   An anointing in which a person is given a supernatural insight into someone's life, into a group, or into a situation.

15   *Wisdom* (1 Corinthians 12.8)   An anointing in which a person is empowered to say just the right thing, to just the right person, at just the right time.

16   *Faith* (1 Corinthians 12.9, 13.2)   An anointing in which a person is given special confidence and conviction that God will achieve what seems, from a human point of view, to be impossible.

17   *Miracles* (1 Corinthians 12.10)   An anointing in which a person is actually empowered by the Spirit to be a channel through which the seemingly impossible is achieved.

18   *Tongues* (1 Corinthians 12.10)   An anointing in which a person is given a new language by the Holy Spirit, either for personal or for public use.

19   *Interpretation* (1 Corinthians 12.10, 30)   An anointing in which a person is enabled to translate a public message uttered in tongues.

20   *Healing* (1 Corinthians 12.9, 30)   An anointing in which a person is empowered by God to minister healing to those suffering from physical, emotional or spiritual affliction.

21   *Discernment* (1 Corinthians 12.10)   An anointing in which a person is equipped to know when someone's words or actions

are motivated by the Holy Spirit, their human spirit or by unholy spirits.

I am constantly reminded by the golden lampstands that it is right to petition for these gifts as the need arises. In other words, it is right to ask for certain gifts for myself when it is obvious that I cannot minister effectively without them.

Character as Well as Charisma

The gifts of the Spirit are sometimes called *charismata* in the New Testament. They are anointings of power which enable us to do the works of Jesus in both the Church and the world. As such, they are spiritual enablements, or supernatural endowments. They speak to us of God's grace (*charis-mata*) and God's power.

But God is interested in our character as well as in our charisma. He is concerned about our level of holiness as well as about our level of power. This means that our petition for spiritual needs must not only include the gifts of the Spirit. It must also include the fruit of the Spirit: 'love, joy, peace, patience, kindness, goodness, faithfulness, gentleness and self-control' (Galatians 5.22–3). Indeed, these characteristics are to form a regular part of our spiritual petitions as we seek to grow more and more into the likeness of Jesus Christ.

The same goes for other lists of spiritual qualities in the New Testament. We can pray for 'compassion, humility, forgiveness' (Colossians 3.12–14), for 'devotion, zeal, servant hearts, faithfulness in prayer, hospitality, the ability to associate with the lowly' (Romans 12.9–16), for 'perseverance under trial, strength to resist temptation, the ability to listen well, obedience in action, control of the tongue, a practical concern for the lonely and the bereaved' (James 1.12–27). Any one of these holiness codes can form the basis of petitionary prayer. Indeed, which one of us does *not* need to cultivate these virtues?

Intimacy is the Highest Goal

The greatest of all spiritual petitions is neither for gifts nor for fruit but for deeper intimacy with Jesus Christ. Jesus himself taught us the importance of intimacy when he commanded us to abide or, more accurately, to 'remain' (*menein*) in the vine (John 15.1–8). The true vine is the Lord Jesus Christ. We are the branches. Our role is to make sure that we stay closely connected and attached to the vine of his presence. This, of course, means a daily discipline of prayer, both the structured prayer described in this book, and the ongoing practice of his divine presence throughout the rest of the day. Prayer is the means, intimacy is the end.

Such a petition for intimacy with God through Jesus Christ is perfectly expressed in the famous hymn by William Cowper,

> O for a closer walk with God,
> A calm and heavenly frame;
> A light to shine upon the road
> That leads me to the Lamb!

These are the words of a person who longs with a holy passion for a greater intimacy with Jesus. They are reminiscent of the words of another great hymn writer, indeed the hymn writer for the Temple in Jerusalem:

> One thing I *ask* of the Lord,
>   this is what I *seek*;
> that I may dwell in the house of the Lord
>   all the days of my life,
> to gaze upon the beauty of the Lord
>   and to see him in his Temple (Psalm 27.4).

There can be no higher form of asking, seeking and knocking than this.

So spend some time at the golden lampstands, praying for greater intimacy, reality and fruitfulness in your relationship with

Jesus. We are the branches, he is the true vine of eternity. Just so long as we are drawing daily on the sap of his Spirit we will grow and flourish.

The Golden Altar of Incense

A large part of our ministry in the sanctuary is thus taken up with petitionary prayer – asking God to meet our physical, emotional and spiritual needs. Here is the place where we can cry out to God to help us meet the bills, to give us faith for giving, to increase our mercy towards the poor, to walk with us in our dark night of the soul, to turn our tears into smiles, to bless our relationships. It is a place where the Father loves to hear about our needs even though he already knows what they are.

Even so, we must recognize that the main focus of the holy place was not the table of shewbread. Nor was it the ten golden lampstands. The main focus was the golden altar of incense at the very end of the sanctuary. This was one of two altars in the Temple. The first was a place of sacrifice and was made of bronze. This was situated in the heart of the court of the priests. The second was a place of intercession and was made of gold. It was situated right in front of the veil which separated the holy place from the holy of holies.

The instructions for the making of this altar were given by the Lord to Moses:

> Make an altar of acacia wood for burning incense. It is to be square, a cubit long and a cubit wide, and two cubits high – its horns of one piece with it. Overlay the top and all the sides and the horns with pure gold, and make a gold moulding around it. . . . Put the altar in front of the curtain that is before the Ark of the Testimony – before the atonement cover that is over the Testimony – where I will meet with you. Aaron must burn fragrant incense on the altar every morning when he tends the lamps. He must burn incense again when he lights the lamps at twilight so that incense will burn regularly before the Lord for generations to come (Exodus 30.1–6).

The Prayers of the Saints

The incense has a specific symbolism. In both the Old and the New Testaments, the incense which rose to the heavens through the roof of the Temple represented the prayers of the saints (living and departed), offered both in the morning and the evening. Thus, in Psalm 141.2, David cries:

> May my prayer be set before you
> like incense;
> May the lifting up of my hands
> be like the evening sacrifice.

In the New Testament, we are actually given a vision of the prayers of God's people as they ascend like incense to God's throne:

> Another angel, who had a golden censer, came and stood at the altar. He was given much incense to offer, with the prayers of all the saints, on the golden altar before the throne. The smoke

96

of the incense, together with the prayers of the saints, went up before God from the angel's hand. Then the angel took the censer, filled it with fire from the altar, and hurled it on the earth; and there came peals of thunder, rumblings, flashes of lightning and an earthquake (Revelation 8.3–5).

The Ministry of Intercession

For me the incense on the altar of the sanctuary represents the intercessions of God's people. Intercessory prayer is to be distinguished from petitionary prayer. Petitionary prayer is praying for my needs. Intercessory prayer is praying for the needs of others. So while the shewbread and the lampstands remind me of God's call to prayer for myself, the golden altar of incense reminds me of God's call to prayer for the Church and for the world.

In this ministry of intercession, I like to picture the fire of God's Spirit descending upon the censer of my heart and igniting the raw material of my prayer into a fragrant offering. I like to picture my intercessions ascending through the roof of the Temple, up to the very throne of God in the heavenly places. I like to picture the fragility of these frail whisps of prayer, and the power of God's response: 'there came peals of thunder, rumblings, flashes of lightning and an earthquake!' I know that my prayers are heard. Not only are they heard, they are also answered – and often with a force that is far stronger than the feeble effort of my heart.

The Importance of Intercession

Why do we need to spend time in the priestly ministry of intercession?

Romans 8 is the richest resource for understanding why intercessory prayer is so necessary. In verses 18 to 39 Paul provides a magnificent description of the relationship between the creation and the Creator. The cosmos is not the same as God, as in pantheism.

But the cosmos is not unrelated to God, as in deism. Rather, the Holy Spirit is at work within the cosmos, and the Holy Spirit is the immanent presence of the transcendent Creator. This means that the cosmos is inhabited by God's presence, but that God is still simultaneously beyond it. He is both in the world and outside it at the same time. The go-between, as it were, is the Holy Spirit.

Paul's charismatic understanding of the relationship between creation and Creator is therefore a subtle one. He knows that the world was subjected to destruction through the Fall, but he also knows that the coming of Jesus has brought a new force into the universe. This force is not some nebulous energy but rather the presence of the kingdom of God, inaugurated on planet earth in the ministry of the historical Jesus. Since the coming of Jesus, the Holy Spirit has been at work restoring the fallen and decaying fabric of the cosmos. He has been intimately and passionately involved in every part of the created order, repairing the ubiquitous damage of the Fall, and helping the world on its new journey towards that end-point when the kingdom of God will be fully established here on earth.

In the meantime we live between the arrival of the kingdom (the first coming of Jesus) and its final consummation (the second coming of Jesus). In this eschatological tension, there is still much suffering in the world. The creation has not yet been fully liberated from its bondage to decay nor from its deep groaning caused by man's first disobedience. There are still floods, famines, earthquakes and diseases.

It is for this reason that the ministry of intercession is still necessary. To be sure, intercessory prayer will disappear when the Lord Jesus Christ returns. What need of intercession will we have where there are no more disasters, no more hospitals, no more funerals and no more tears? But that day is in the future. So in the meantime, there is great need for intercessory prayer. God has given us the task of intercessory prayer as one of the instruments by which his providence comes into being on earth. Until God's perfect future is an eternal present, intercessory prayer will consequently be essential.

The Theology of Intercession

However, while it is easy to see the relevance of intercessory prayer, many of us struggle to know what actually to pray. Here again, Romans 8 comes to the rescue. In verses 26 and 27, Paul rightly says that we do not know what we ought to pray for. We are, in short, stuck. We see the need to pray; we may even see the needs which need praying for. But the actual performance of intercession brings us up short. We are straightaway confronted by a sense of inadequacy. What do we actually say? How do we know that we are in alignment with God's providence?

It is at this point that Paul brings us some words of encouragement. He assures us that the same Holy Spirit who is at work within the created order comes to our aid. The Spirit helps us in our weakness. He himself intercedes for us 'with groans that words cannot express'. He himself intercedes for the saints *in us*, and in accordance with God's will.

What is going on when the Spirit helps us in this way? Put simply, the Holy Spirit, at the moment of our speechlessness, gathers us up and joins our minds with that of the Ascended Lord Jesus. Jesus, we read in Romans 8.34, is he who died, who was raised to life, and who is now at the right hand of God *interceding for us*. So when we enter into intercessory prayer, the Holy Spirit lifts us up into the presence of the Ascended Christ, and joins our prayers with his. The Holy Spirit incorporates us in that constant stream of prayer which is going on in heaven – prayer which is ministered by the Son to the Father. This means that, in our priestly ministry of intercession, the Holy Spirit joins us with the ministry of our Great High Priest. He helps us to know the mind of Christ, who is the 'Intercessor, Friend of Sinners' (1 Corinthians 2.6–16).

The Fire of Intercession

If this Pauline theology reveals anything it is the importance of praying in the Spirit rather than in the flesh. If we are to intercede with the mind of Christ, we must allow the Holy Spirit to ignite our hearts so that he can pray in us and through us the prayers of the Ascended Lord. Maybe this is one reason why Paul is so insistent, 'Pray in the Spirit on all occasions' (Ephesians 6.18). But how do we do this? It is all very well understanding the principle of anointed intercession. It is quite another thing actually doing it!

At this point we need to spend some time looking at the place of silence and listening. So far in this book I have stressed the importance of vocalizing our thanksgiving, our praise, our penitence. I find it particularly helpful (as an aid to concentration) to do this out loud. However, the more contemplative readers will be asking, 'Doesn't this model of prayer involve an awful lot of talking? Are there not enough words already in our lives? Where's the place of silence and of listening prayer?' If that is a question you have been asking, then I have to respond by saying that silence and listening are essential before intercessory prayer. Ecclesiastes 5.1–2 warns us:

> Guard your steps
>> when you go to the house of God.
> Go near to listen
>> rather than to offer the sacrifice of fools,
>> who do not know that they do wrong.
>
> Do not be quick with your mouth,
>> do not be hasty in your heart
>> to utter anything before God.
> God is in heaven
>> and you are on earth,
>> so let your words be few.

Before the altar of incense, a contemplative commitment to silence is extremely important before embarking on prayer for others.

The Power of Intercession

After a period of silence, I often find that I start to receive a burden for a person or a place, or a series of burdens for people and places.

It is extremely important at this point to be alert to the whispering of the Spirit.

Just occasionally they are hard to miss. David Brainerd, the great eighteenth-century missionary, once had a day which was remarkable for its profound burdens. Johnathan Edwards wrote up his life and diary, and in an entry for 1742, when Brainerd was only twenty-four, we read of three anointings for prayer; one before noon, one in the afternoon, one at night:

> In the forenoon, I felt the power of intercession for the advancement of the kingdom of my dear Lord and Saviour in the world; and withal, a most sweet resignation, and even consolation and joy in the thoughts of suffering hardships, distresses, and even death itself, in the promotion of it.
>
> In the afternoon, God was with me of a truth. Oh, it was a blessed company indeed! My soul was drawn out very much for the world; I think I had more enlargement for sinners, than for the children of God; though I felt as if I could spend my life in cries for both.
>
> Just at night the Lord visited me marvellously in prayer: I think my soul never was in such agony before. I felt no restraint; for the treasures of divine grace were opened to me. I wrestled for absent friends, for the ingathering of souls, and for the children of God in many distant places.[2]

This kind of anointing is, of course, the exception rather than the rule. In reality, a burden for specific prayer is far less overwhelming and, in my experience, a great deal more impressionistic. Usually the leading of the Spirit is discerned as we start to catch glimpses of faces in our mind's eye. In between these 'flash photographs', it is helpful to mention the names of the people who are brought to mind, and then to allow the Spirit to do the sighing, the groaning, the speaking, in a language which is not our own. When we do this, we let go of the raft of our own agenda and allow ourselves to enter a stream of divine consciousness – the mind of the Ascended Christ, our Great High Priest.

The Levels of Intercession

Usually I try to do this within a structure. Since I am committed to praying for the far as well as the near, I like to keep in mind a structure which begins at the most immediate level, and then extends outwards to the furthest parts of the world.

So I begin by praying in the Spirit for my *church*. Here I allow the Spirit to direct me into that stream of divine consciousness which I have just mentioned. Often I am surprised by the faces which come into my mind. Just occasionally I sense God's leading to visit someone, or an intuition about what is really happening in someone's marriage or home. Sometimes I receive the first glimmers of a new goal or vision for the Church, or a reminder of work left undone. Whatever the case, this is where I start, interceding in the Spirit for the local church where I serve.

The next level involves praying in the Spirit for my *community*. Here I allow the Spirit to give me a burden for a local school, a pub, a group of people, a housing estate, a particular street, another church, a hospital, whatever. Almost always there is a sense of the Spirit wanting to mediate the healing presence of God to the houses, streets and estates in the community. Sometimes I will get a sense of illumination about the social, structural and spiritual forces which are contributing towards a hitherto unexplained resistance to the Gospel. In any event, I will seek to pray 'Your kingdom come' in the community where I live.

The third level of prayer involves the *city*. I am particularly blessed in that my sitting room window overlooks the entire city of Sheffield. Often I get a sense of the Lord Jesus weeping over the city of Sheffield as he did over the city of Jerusalem. This underlines the need to pray for our cities. Again we need to allow the Spirit to lead us to those parts of the city where our prayers will be most beneficial. As in the community, there are strategic people and places that need to be stormed and transformed through militant, loving prayer. Only the Spirit can reveal what those key targets are.

The fourth level moves beyond the city to the *country*. In 1 Timothy 2.1–4, the writer says,

> I urge, then, first of all, that requests, prayers, intercession and thanksgiving be made for everyone – for kings and all those in authority, that we may live peaceful and quiet lives in all godliness and holiness. This is good, and pleases God our Saviour, who wants all men to be saved and to come to a knowledge of the truth.

Here we are urged to make sure that our intercessions are not restricted but rather wide-angled in focus. Praying for the royal family, for the government of our nation, for the institutions and agencies which wield power and influence (particularly the economy and the media), for various professions (especially teachers and the world of education), for topical issues (such as Sunday trading, abortion, and so on), is vital. Again we must allow the Spirit to lead us to those national concerns which are on the heart of God.

The fifth level moves from the country to the *continents*. Here we are in real danger of moving into the kind of vague praying which we try to avoid. My own conviction is that God wants to give every praying Christian a burden for at least one specific country or continent, or for one particular missionary organization or missionary. If every praying Christian allowed the Spirit to give them one such burden, which then resulted in fervent and specific prayer, the impact on the world would, I believe, be profound and lasting. So permit the Spirit to give you that burden. Do not try to take on too much. The Flash Gordon approach to personal prayer ('Fourteen minutes to save the universe!') usually degenerates into meaningless platitudes.

The final level of intercessory prayer moves from the continents to the whole of *creation*. As Christians, we need to remember that the same Holy Spirit is at work in both us and the evolving cosmos. Romans 8 proves that conclusively. Indeed, both Christians and creation 'groan inwardly' in the eschatological tension between the now and the not yet of God's kingdom (Romans 8.22–3). God's ultimate purposes therefore include both planet earth and humanity. That being so, Christians can express their solidarity with creation through prayer for the healing of the land.

The healing of the land is important to God (2 Chronicles 7.14); it was a vital part of ancient Jewish culture (the *birkat ha-'ares* or 'blessing of the land'); it was important to the Celtic Christian missionaries who Christianized so much of pagan Britain. It should be an important ministry for us today. So spend time in prayer for the healing of creation, with specific prayer for the land in your locality, and for those aspects of creation that are oppressed and threatened (Numbers 35.33; 2 Samuel 21.14).

The Tears of Intercession

For most of us, intercessory prayer will be a ministry just like this: praying through matters related to the Church, community, city, country, continents and creation, guided (we trust) by the impressions of the Spirit. This ministry involves silence, in so far as we have to listen to the subliminal promptings of the Spirit. It involves some speaking, in so far as we pray either in human words or in tongues for those whom the Spirit brings to remembrance.

But there are those whom God takes into a deeper form of intercessory prayer which involves neither words nor tongues, but rather tears. Yesterday evening in the church where I work, I was praying for a woman who came to me very troubled. She had entered a season of her life where she seemed to be living with an awful lot of grief. Some of it was about herself and her family. But most of it was for others around her in the Church and for the Church itself. Much of her time was spent with a feeling of dereliction and apparent Godforsakenness for which she felt guilty. As three of us prayed for her, I began to see a picture developing before my eyes which I shared with her out loud, as it became clearer:

> I can see a great expanse of desert land. It's white with heat and it's very flat. There is absolutely no vegetation there.
>
> In the centre of my vision, I can see you. You are standing before an altar made of sand and stone. Your hands are outstretched towards heaven and you are pleading with God on

behalf of those whom you know. There is a look of desolation in your face.

As you pray, I see streams of tears pouring down your face. As these tears fall to the ground, I see flowers blooming, trees growing, pools of water appearing in every part of the desert. I see the desert turning into a garden.

At the same time I see people emerging out of the desert sand, where they have been buried in a kind of living death. The life is returning to their faces. They are smelling the flowers, drinking the water and basking in the shade of the trees.

The more your tears flow, the more the land is blessed, and the more the people are healed.

The vision stopped at this point, and as it did, I began to interpret to her what I sensed God might be saying:

You should not feel guilty about these tears. They are a grace-gift from heaven. The Lord has given you these tears as a form of prayer. Indeed, these tears are the deepest form of prayer. So when you weep, know that you are closer to God than at any other time. You are right in the centre of God's heart, which weeps with compassion for those whose lives are empty and bruised. So let the tears flow. Let the Spirit intercede through you with these tears. And the Lord will turn your grief into joy, your sorrow into dancing.

This incident has shown me once and for all how precious tears are to God. Indeed, there can be no more precious form of prayer than the kind of intercessory weeping which God has given to this woman of God. If you have been given the tears of intercession, regard it as a privilege as well as a challenge.

The Mystery of Intercession

We cannot end this chapter on petitionary and intercessory prayer without giving some attention to one of the great mysteries of the Christian life – unanswered prayer. Sometimes we have to say, with complete honesty, that having prayed with the most fervent words and with the most desperate tears there appears to be no change. The person is not healed. A marriage partner is not provided. Our Church is not renewed. Our pleading at the altar of incense seems to have been to no avail.

There may be a number of reasons for this. Sometimes we have simply not persevered in prayer. We were supposed to knock loudly and persistently on the doors of heaven and instead we only tapped once (Luke 18.1–8). At other times we have under-estimated the need for warfare prayer (Ephesians 6.10–18). In other words, we have not seen the level of spiritual oppression in a situation. Instead of hitting enemy tanks with a barrage of constant prayer, we have sought to destroy them with occasional 'arrow prayers'. No wonder little change has occurred!

Sometimes we have simply failed to align ourselves with God's will. In other words, we have asked for the wrong things. We have allowed the desires of our flesh to dictate the how and the what of our prayers. For example, the mother of St Augustine pleaded with God to stop her son from leaving home and travelling to Rome. Yet Augustine left, and on that journey a far greater dream was fulfilled for his mother; Augustine was converted. Later, he wrote about this incident as follows:

> O Lord, in your wisdom, you granted the substance of my mother's desire. You refused the things she prayed for, in order that you might effect in me what she had always wanted. She loved to keep me with her, as mothers are wont to do. In fact, far more than most mothers. But she did not know what joy you were preparing for her as a result of my desertion! (*Confessions*).

In the final analysis, God must be seen as completely sovereign in the matter of prayer. I have seen God heal the sick. I have also sensed him say, 'This sickness is unto death'. I have seen God say 'yes' to my prayers. I have also heard him say 'not yet' and even 'no'. Sometimes God has answered prayers that have been mere wishful sighs – not even half-prayers in any orthodox sense. At other times he has refused to answer the most poignant pleas. The important thing is not to allow the mystery of God's sovereignty to stop us from praying. God calls us to the table of shewbread and to the golden lampstands. He calls us to petitionary prayer. He also calls us to the altar of incense, to the ministry of intercessory prayer. As priests of the kingdom, these are essential ministries. God calls us to 'pray constantly' (1 Thessalonians 5.17) and not to give up.

As we read in Leviticus 6.13: 'The fire must be kept burning on the altar continuously; it must not go out'.

PRAYER

O Lord, I climb the steps to the holy place. Thank you for giving me access to your sanctuary through the death and resurrection of your Son, our Great High Priest.

I pause in the porch out of reverence for your holiness . . .

I now stand before the golden table of shewbread. Thank you for encouraging us to pray, 'Give us this day our daily bread'. Thank you that you are a Father who welcomes our asking, encourages our seeking, answers our knocking. Today I ask you to help me with the following needs that are much on my heart . . .

Lord, I come now to the golden lampstands. I thank you that you want to help me to minister effectively today. Increase in me the spiritual gifts of . . . and draw me closer to yourself, through Jesus.

And now I come to the golden altar of incense. Help me in the silence now to hear what you are saying and to know the mind of Christ . . .

Silence and listening . . .

I pray first of all for our church . . .

I pray for our community . . .

I pray for our city . . .

A KINGDOM OF PRIESTS

I pray for the country . . .

I pray for the continents of the world . . .

I pray for your creation . . .

Lord, in your mercy, hear my prayer. In Jesus' name. Amen.

5

THE HOLY OF HOLIES

'Prayer ushers us into the Holy of Holies where we bow before the deepest mysteries of the faith'.

Richard Foster, *Prayer*

The Innermost Sanctuary

We are now nearing the end of our journey into God's presence. We began in Chapter 1 with the gates of thanksgiving, and looked at the eucharistic ministry of thanksgiving prayer. In Chapter 2 we proceeded through the gates into the court of praise where we explored how to worship the Father and the Son with the prayer of the mind, the prayer of the heart and the prayer of the spirit. In Chapter 3 we paused at the altar of sacrifice and defined the ministry of confession. We then entered the holy place in Chapter 4, and examined the two ministries of petition (the table of shewbread and the golden lampstands) and of intercession (the golden altar of incense). Now we stand before the veil which was used to separate the holy from the most holy place of all.

We read in 1 Kings 6.19 of Solomon's construction of the innermost sanctuary of the Temple:

> Solomon prepared the inner sanctuary within the Temple to set the ark of the covenant of the Lord there. The inner sanctuary was twenty cubits long, twenty wide and twenty high. He overlaid the inside with pure gold, and he also overlaid the altar of cedar.

A few verses later, the narrator describes the interior of the holy of holies:

> In the inner sanctuary Solomon made a pair of cherubim of olive wood, each ten cubits high. One wing of the first cherub was five cubits long, and the other wing five cubits – ten cubits from wing tip to wing tip. The second cherub also measured ten cubits, for the two cherubim were identical in size and shape. The height of each cherub was ten cubits. He placed the cherubim inside the innermost room of the Temple, with their wings spread out. The wing of one cherub touched one wall, while the wing of the other touched the other wall, and their wings touched each other in the middle of the room. He overlaid the cherubim with gold.

110

When the great day came and the Temple was completed, the ark of the covenant was brought into the holy of holies:

> The priests then brought the ark of the Lord's covenant to its place in the inner sanctuary of the Temple, the Most Holy Place, and put it beneath the cherubim. The cherubim spread their wings over the place of the ark and overshadowed the ark and its carrying poles. . . . When the priests withdrew from the Holy Place, the cloud filled the Temple of the Lord. And the priests could not perform their service because of the cloud, for the glory of the Lord filled his Temple (1 Kings 8.6–11).

The Place of God's Throne

It was not long before this innermost sanctuary was seen as the earthly counterpart of God's throne in heaven. This is hardly surprising. The ark of the covenant looked like a throne and was even called 'the cherub throne'. The gold floor and walls were seen as symbolic of God's royalty. The cherubim – celestial angels – were regarded as the concrete counterparts of the angels which surrounded the throne of God in heaven. Very soon there developed a belief that the only source of illumination in the most holy place was the *kabod Yahweh*, the shekinah glory of the Lord. While the court of praise was illuminated by the sun, and the holy place by candlelight, the innermost sanctuary was believed to be illuminated by the radiant presence of the Lord himself. No wonder the people of God saw the holy of holies as a counterpart of the very heart of the heavenly city, where the Lord reigns in majesty. As Jeremiah said, 'A glorious throne set on high from the beginning is the place of our sanctuary' (Jeremiah 17.12). As God says to Ezekiel, from deep within the Temple, 'Son of man, this is the place of my throne and the place for the soles of my feet' (Ezekiel 43.7).

Thus it was that the innermost sanctuary came to symbolize eternal realities. It pointed to that transcendent realm where the King of Kings was believed to reign in glory, seated between the cherubim, the angels of heaven. As King David put it:

The Lord reigns,
    let the nations tremble;
he sits enthroned between the cherubim,
    let the earth shake.
Great is the Lord in Zion;
    he is exalted over all the nations.
Let them praise your great and awesome name –
    he is holy.
The King is mighty, he loves justice –
    you have established equity;
in Jacob you have done
    what is just and right.
Exalt the Lord our God,
    and worship at his footstool;
    he is holy (Psalm 99.1–5).

Visions of the Throne

Over the centuries, the vision of God's throne, inspired by the holy of holies, became a frequent theme of apocalyptic literature – writings in which the holy prophets saw the hidden world of heaven. Some of these visions are in the Bible, others are recorded in Jewish literature contemporary with the Bible. As Margaret Barker writes, 'From the time of Isaiah right through until the Book of Revelation, there was a continuous tradition of throne visions'.[1]

These visions of the throne, inspired by the Temple, are beautifully graphic:[2]

In the year that King Uzziah died, I saw the Lord seated on a throne, high and exalted, and the train of his robe filled the temple. Above him were seraphs, each with six wings. With two wings they covered their faces, with two they covered their feet, and with two they were flying. And they were calling to one another, 'Holy, holy, holy is the Lord Almighty; the whole earth is full of his glory'. At the sound of their voices the doorposts and thresholds shook and the temple was filled with smoke (Isaiah 6.1–3).

112

THE HOLY OF HOLIES

As I looked, thrones were placed, and one that was ancient of days took his seat; his raiment was white as snow, and the hair of his head like pure wool; his throne was fiery flames, its wheels were burning fire. A stream of fire issued and came forth from before him; a thousand thousands served him, and ten thousand times ten thousand stood before him; the court sat in judgement, and the books were opened . . . (Daniel 7.9–10).

The following example is from outside the Bible, from a Jewish document known as *1 Enoch* (roughly contemporary with the Book of Daniel). In it, Enoch is described having a vision of the heavenly Temple and the throne of God within the most holy place:

> And as I shook and trembled I fell upon my face and saw a vision. And behold there was an opening before me and a second house which is greater than the former and everything was built with tongues of fire. And in every respect it excelled the other . . . in glory and great honour . . . to the extent that it is imposs- ible to recount to you concerning its glory and greatness. As for its floor, it was of fire and above it was lightning and the path of the stars; and as for the ceiling it was flaming fire. And I observed and saw inside it a lofty throne . . . its appearance was like crystal and its wheels like the shining sun; and I heard the voice of the cherubim; and from beneath the throne were issuing streams of living fire. It was difficult to look at. And the Great Glory was sitting upon it . . . as for his gown, which was shining more brightly than the sun, it was whiter than any snow. None of the angels was able to come in and see the face of the Excellent and Glorious One, and no one of the flesh can see him. The flaming fire was around him and a great fire stood before him
> (*1 Enoch* 14.8–22).

Another example can be found in *The Apocalypse of Abraham* (again, not in the Bible):

> And while I was standing and watching, I saw behind the living creatures a chariot with fiery wheels. Each wheel was full of eyes round about. And above the wheels was the throne which I had

seen. And it was covered with fire and the fire circled it round about, and an indescribable light surrounded the fiery cloud (*Apocalypse of Abraham* 18.12–13).

Two final examples are from *The Songs of the Sabbath Sacrifice*, which were discovered at both Qumran and Massada. These songs were sung by Jews in first-century Palestine:

> The cherubim bless the image of the throne chariot above the firmament and they praise the majesty of the luminous firmament beneath his glory seat. When the wheels advance, angels of holiness come and go. From between his glorious wheels there is as it were a fiery vision of most holy spirits. About them the appearance of rivulets of fire in the likeness of gleaming brass, and a work of . . . radiance in many-coloured glory, marvellous pigments, clearly mingled.

> At their marvellous stations are spirits, many-coloured like the work of a weaver, splendid engraved figures. In the midst of a glorious appearance of scarlet, colours of the most spiritual light, they hold to their station before the King, spirits of pure colours in the midst of an appearance of whiteness. The likeness of the glorious spirit is like a work of art of a weaver. These are the Princes of those marvellously clothed for service, the Princes of the Kingdom, the kingdom of the holy ones of the King of holiness in all the heights of the sanctuaries of his glorious kingdom.

The Ultimate Revelation

It is the imagery of these visions which lies behind much of the strange sights recorded in the Book of Revelation, the climactic book of the New Testament. Here we see how central the furniture of the earthly Temple is to John's description of heaven. Indeed, the setting for the whole book seems to be the Temple in Jerusalem. John describes a seven-branched *menorah* (1.12; 4.5), an altar where incense is offered (5.8; 6.9; 8.3–5), a great sea of crystal before the throne (reminiscent of the bronze sea, 4.6) and the ark of the covenant (Revelation 11.19).

The focal point of everything in Revelation is the throne of God, which is again reminiscent of the cherub throne in the inner sanctuary. John portrays this part of heaven in the most majestic terms. In Revelation 4 we are given a brief but awesome glimpse of the worship of God which has been taking place since the very beginning of time, and which will go on for eternity. In many ways it is the most spectacular and the most dramatic vision of the throne of God.

This chapter of Revelation is extremely pertinent for our final ministry as priests of the kingdom of God. Once we enter through the veil and kneel in the holy of holies we are in the presence of the One who was, who is, who is to come, the Almighty (Revelation 1.8). After all our thanking, praising, confessing, petitioning and interceding, we pause now to worship God in all his infinite glory. Here we come before the throne of God and worship at his footstool. Here we enjoy the most beautiful of all the spiritual disciplines: beholding the throne in devotional prayer.[3]

The Transcendence of God

This discipline involves a fixed attention upon the sovereignty of God. It is a vital discipline because many of us have lost that awareness of the transcendence of God which is so vividly captured in Revelation 4. The *Chambers Dictionary* defines the word 'transcendent' as 'superior or supreme in excellence'. It defines the verb 'transcend' as 'to rise above', and 'to pass or lie beyond the limit of . . .' When I speak of the transcendence of God I mean his super-eminent otherness. I mean that aspect of his being which is mysterious, fearful, beyond our reason and our understanding.

The word 'transcendence' is often used in contrast to the word 'immanence'. People speak of both the transcendence of God and of his immanence. This second word refers to the indwelling, pervading presence of God in creation and in believers. When people speak of the transcendent God they are referring to the

God who is beyond us. When they speak of the immanent God they are referring to the God who is within us.

The biblical revelation of God holds both of these truths together. The Bible shows that God is first of all immanent. With the birth of Jesus, God has truly become present with us. He is 'Immanuel', 'God with us'. With the outpouring of the Holy Spirit at Pentecost, things have gone one stage further. For Christians it is true that God is not only 'with us' but 'in us'. The presence of the Holy Spirit in our lives is the immanence of Almighty God.

However, just because God is now with us and in us, this does not mean that he is no longer beyond us. One of the main reasons why the Book of Revelation is so important to the New Testament is because it reminds us that God is not only immanent below but also transcendent above. He is not only on the throne of our hearts (hopefully) but also on the throne of heaven, reigning in immortal splendour.

The Loss of Transcendence

In many parts of the Western Church, the immanence of God is emphasized more than his transcendence. This is particularly true of contemporary charismatic churches. The prevailing theology of the charismatic movement tends to stress the experience of God the Holy Spirit. As John McKay has written, 'No charismatic would feel at home with the kind of biblical interpretation that speaks simply of "the supernatural", "the divine", "the numinous", "the transcendent", or that would seek to interpret all in terms of purely human understanding, scientific thought, or philosophy. To him God is Father, Lord and King, and is very near and very personal'.[4]

There are positive side-effects of such an immanent understanding of God, not least that of rescuing God from an ivory tower of remote unreality. However, such a theology will always be incomplete if it is not balanced with an authentic understanding of God's transcendence. As Richard Lovelace has said, 'One of the most hopeful contributions of the Charismatic renewal movement

116

has been . . . its insistence on the experience of God's presence in a context of worship and prayer. But unless the God who is worshipped is the awesome, holy, sovereign lord of Scripture, even this approach cannot continue to serve as a catalyst for spiritual life'.[5]

The Michael Fagin syndrome

The importance of this truth can be illustrated in this way. About ten years ago a man called Michael Fagin climbed over the walls of the Buckingham Palace grounds, broke into the palace itself, found his way into the Queen's bedroom, and then sat on her bed smoking and chatting with her. The Queen was able to raise the alarm and the man was eventually arrested. However, by this time he had made his point. He had proved that it was possible to break into the palace and to invade the Queen's privacy.

It could be argued that there is a Michael Fagin syndrome in some contemporary Western Christianity. Many of us forget, as we approach God in worship, that he is the King of Eternity, that he is far greater than anything or anyone we can ever imagine. Speaking for myself, there have been many times when I have broken into the palace of God's presence rather than entered with reverence and humility. There have been times when I have sat and chatted rather than knelt and listened. On those occasions I have not been obedient to God's Word in Hebrews 12.28–9: 'Let us worship God acceptably with reverence and awe, for our God is a consuming fire'.

Learning from the East

Here we have much to learn from our brothers and sisters in the Eastern Orthodox Church. In Orthodox worship there is a great deal of emphasis upon the Holy Spirit and upon the experience of God. But a primary theme of Orthodox theology is also the infinite majesty and transcendence of God. As Bishop Kallistos of Diokletia writes:

> We approach the living God 'in fear and trembling', 'in love and awe'. Negative or apophatic language is used to underline the divine transcendence: God's power is 'indescribable' and his

goodness 'unutterable'; 'your glory cannot be approached . . . no one has ever seen you nor is able to see you . . . who alone are holy, immeasurable and beyond human expression . . . incomprehensible in being'. Such language, so far from being an empty formality, expresses a vivid, inescapable conviction pervading all Orthodox theology.[6]

The conviction of the Orthodox Christian is therefore this: that God is both near and far, with us and beyond us, immanent and transcendent. He is on the one hand the core of everything, closer to us than our own heart. That is why an Orthodox service will begin with an invocation of the Holy Spirit, who is 'everywhere present and filling all things'. On the other hand, God is seen as beyond us. So the same service will contain prayers which focus upon the transcendent throne of God:

> Around your throne in heaven
> angelic powers exalt you
> with ceaseless hymns
> and unending songs of praise;
> so may your praise be ever on our lips
> that we may proclaim
> the greatness of your holy Name.[7]

What is so attractive about Orthodox spirituality is therefore that it is integrative; it combines a theology of God's immanence with a theology of God's transcendence.

The God who is Good but not Safe

Why is it, then, that so much Western spirituality is resistant to the idea of the holy otherness of God? This resistance is, after all, a recent, twentieth-century phenomenon. Look at any traditional hymn book and you will find plenty of hymns whose poetic descriptions of the throne of God evoke a sense of wonder:

Jesus, where'er Thy people meet,

There they behold Thy mercy-seat;
Where'er they seek Thee Thou art found
And every place is hallowed ground (William Cowper, 1769).

My God, how wonderful Thou art,
Thy majesty how bright,
How beautiful Thy mercy-seat
In depths of burning light! (F. W. Faber, 1849).

O worship the Lord in the beauty of holiness!
Bow down before Him, His glory proclaim:
With gold of obedience and incense of lowliness
Kneel and adore Him; the Lord is His name (J.S.B. Monsell, 1863).

These words take us right into the innermost sanctuary of God's presence to behold the throne of grace. They show that there have been times in Western Christianity when churches have been receptive rather than resistant to an emphasis upon transcendence.

So why is there such an overemphasis upon God's immanence these days? Part of the answer is that we have married the spirit of the age and produced a comfortable Christianity in which the disturbing aspects of God have been glossed over. We have produced a God who is safe and in the process we have forgotten – as the saying goes – that Jesus Christ came not only to comfort the afflicted but to afflict the comfortable. We have neglected subjects like the righteous anger of God and this has produced an erosion of the sense of God's holiness in both the Church and the world.

In C.S. Lewis' story, *The Lion, the Witch and the Wardrobe*, there is a very revealing exchange between two girls and a Mr and Mrs Beaver. The subject of their conversation is Aslan, a lion who, in C.S. Lewis' tale, symbolizes the Son of God:

> 'Is – is he a man?' asked Lucy.
> 'Aslan a man!' said Mr. Beaver sternly. 'Certainly not. I tell you he is the King of the wood and the son of the great Emperor-Beyond-the-Sea. Don't you know who is the King of Beasts? Aslan is a lion – *the* lion, the great Lion.'

'Ooh!' said Susan, 'I'd thought he was a man. Is he – quite safe? I shall feel rather nervous about meeting a lion.'

'That you will, dearie, and no mistake', said Mrs. Beaver, 'if there's anyone who can appear before Aslan without their knees knocking, they're either braver than most or else just silly.'

'Then he isn't safe?' said Lucy.

'Safe?' said Mr. Beaver. 'Don't you hear what Mrs. Beaver tells you? Who said anything about safe? Course he isn't safe. But he's good. He's the King, I tell you.'[8]

What I like very much about this conversation is the idea that Aslan is good but not necessarily safe. This is a perfect description of God. In the New Testament, there are times when God does not seem to be altogether safe and predictable. For instance, in the Acts of the Apostles we see a God who lifts his Son Jesus into heaven (Acts 1), who shakes buildings and descends on people with tongues of fire (Acts 2), who heals a man crippled from birth (Acts 3), who strikes down those who hold back from giving all (Acts 5), and so on.

The first recorded prayer of the Spirit-filled believers in Acts 4.23–30 shows how the first Christians appreciated this sense of God's otherness. Their prayer begins with the words, 'Sovereign Lord'. The word for 'Sovereign Lord' is *despota* from which we get 'despot'. A despot is someone with absolute power, usually a tyrant! By using the word *despotes*, the believers in Jerusalem were expressing their respect for God, 'the King of Creation (v. 24), the Lord of history (vv. 25–8), and the head of the church (vv. 29–30)'. They were expressing their faith in a God who is good, but not necessarily safe.

Needless to say, there is an urgent need for us to recover this sense of God's greatness in our day.

Beholding the Throne in Prayer

So how can we recapture something of this sense of God's awesome sovereignty in our own times? One answer lies in what we do in the final stage of prayer as priests of the kingdom.

In the fifth and final stage of prayer, we pause at the entrance to the innermost sanctuary, the place associated with the vision of God's throne. Traditionally, a great ornamented veil separated the holy from the most holy place. Once every year the Jewish high priest was permitted to enter through the veil to atone for the sins of the people. Under the new covenant, of course, all this has changed: the death of Jesus has meant that we too can enter the most holy place of God's presence. As a result of Calvary, the veil in the Temple has been torn in two, thereby leaving the entrance to the heart of God wide open for those who believe and trust in Christ. This means that we can have access to the innermost sanctuary; we can walk with reverence into the presence of the King of Kings.

What we do when we enter the innermost sanctuary is to meditate on the throne of God described in Revelation 4. This form of meditation is a concentrated and imaginative focus upon God's royal transcendence as described in Revelation 4. It is a spiritual discipline which is commanded in Scripture. That is why, in Colossians 3.1–3, Paul tells his readers:

> Since, then, you have been raised with Christ, set your hearts on things above, where Christ is seated at the right hand of God. Set your minds on things above, not on earthly things. For you died, and your life is now hidden with Christ in God.

Here the command is to set both heart (emotions) and mind (imagination, reason) upon the heavenly realities where Jesus Christ is enthroned. The command is to meditate on heavenly realities.

The Art of Meditation

Meditating on the throne of God involves a slow reading of Revelation 4 in which we allow each statement to impact us so that we can respond in either silent or vocal worship.

It needs to be said at the outset that this is not an easy discipline to master. In reading the Bible we have become hopelessly handicapped by the principles of the Enlightenment. For centuries we have been reading the Scriptures for information not for trans-

121

formation. In other words, we have been reading them as a source of historical data (mostly disputed) rather than as the Word of God which transforms us. Furthermore, we have been reading the Bible from a perspective of detachment rather than from a perspective of participation. In other words, we have learnt to stand above the text like a scientist examining a cell under a microscope. We have lost the art of being able to enter into the world of the text, to feel the experiences it describes, to identify with the characters depicted, to respond to the signals it elicits.

The problem with a meditative reading of Scripture is that it is entirely the opposite of an Enlightenment hermeneutic. A meditative approach to the Bible requires us to be formed and not just informed. That is, it requires that we give up examining the text in favour of being examined by the text. Furthermore, it requires total participation in the world of the text. Detachment is the last thing which will yield a fruitful response. We must be prepared to enter into the symbolic universe of the Bible, however strange some of those symbols may seem to us today.

In relation to Revelation 4, a meditative reading requires us take each phrase of the chapter, accepting it as a true insight into the heavenly realm, and to allow it to evoke a devotional response from our hearts.

In the following pages, we will take phrases from Revelation 4 and 5 and highlight some of the affective responses which they might encourage as a result of a meditative reading.

After this I looked

In the Ignatian tradition of meditating on Scripture, the human senses play a significant part in the reading process. We are encouraged to smell, to taste, to touch, to hear, and above all to see what the Scriptures describe. The word 'looked' in the opening statement of Revelation 4 alerts us straight away to the need to open the eyes of our imagination. What is about to follow is of a very visual nature. We must therefore activate our imaginations to look with love upon the heavenly realities of John's vision.

Notice that the writer says, 'I looked'. First of all, we should note that this is in the past tense. St John says, 'I looked', not 'I see'. In order for us to register the content of this Scripture as a reality in our own experience we must turn what was past tense for St John into a present tense. From now on I will therefore be referring to the content of Revelation 4 in the present tense.

Secondly, we need to notice the little word 'I' in 'I looked'. St John is emphasizing that the vision was originally a personal experience. This again is important for meditative reading. In meditating upon Revelation 4, it is important to personalize the Scripture; that is, to see the vision as a direct experience for us now. This means that from now on I shall be referring to my own experience as I gaze upon the majesty of God.

There before me is an open door

Doors are powerful symbols. In John 10.7, Jesus says 'I am the door'. In Revelation 3.20, Jesus says, 'Behold! I stand at the door and knock'. Clearly a threshold must be crossed if I am to participate in the heavenly word of Revelation 4.

Entering the open door in heaven is the ultimate liminal experience. The word 'liminal' comes from the Latin '*limen*' meaning 'a threshold'. As I pass through the open door in heaven I see myself at the threshold of eternity. I prepare myself for what Thérèse of Lisieux called 'dreaming of heaven'.[9]

As I start to meditate on this truth, I begin to wonder at the generosity of God. It is an open door to eternity. The door is open wide, not shut. There is a sense of divine invitation and welcome here. God says, 'Come up here, my child'. I respond by walking into what George Ladd called 'the presence of the future'.[10]

At once I am in the Spirit

As soon as I hear these words, I am 'in the Spirit'. Here I pause and reflect on what it means to be 'in the Spirit' in prayer. I remember that the promise of Scripture is that in prayer I am lifted up by the Spirit into the presence of the Ascended Christ. Paul says in Romans 8.26 that we do not know how to pray because we are weak. However, the Holy Spirit helps us in our weakness and intercedes within us. More than that, the Holy Spirit joins our prayer to the prayer of Jesus before the throne of God.

Whether I feel it or not, the fact is I am right now elevated from the frailty of my humanity into the unending dialogue of prayer between the Son and the Father in heaven. According to Romans 8, I experience an ascension of the spirit.

There before me is a throne in heaven

The first sight I see is God's throne. It is a magnificent throne. A huge throne which seems to function as a primary source of light. I cannot make out the form of God upon this throne because light seems to be pouring out of the very centre of it. It is an awesome sight, in many ways so far beyond anything that is describable. Perhaps that is why St John is unusually sparse with his words. All he says is that there is a throne in heaven. All I can do is recognize that I am in the presence of royalty. I am in the presence of the *Pantokrator*, the Almighty, the one who is Lord of history and King of Creation; the one before whom every knee must one day bow.

And there is someone sitting on it

How I admire the reticence of St John! John is so overawed by what he sees that he cannot even name God. He describes God as 'someone sitting on the throne'. He does the same thing in Revelation 4.3 ('The one who sat there'), Revelation 4.9 ('him who sits on the throne'), Revelation 4.10 ('him who sits on the throne'), Revelation 5.1 ('him who sat on the throne'), and Revelation 5.7 ('him who sat on the throne').

Paul Tillich, in a sermon on 'The Divine Name', says that I must treat God as wholly different from other people and other things. As Tillich puts it, 'God would not be God if we could possess him like any object of our familiar world'.[11] This has implications for calling God by name. Although God has given us names for himself, I must use them with 'sacred embarrassment', so as to 'preserve the respectful distance from the Holy-Itself'.[12] As Tillich writes, 'Men have always tried to use the divine name in the same way, not in order to break its power, but to harness its power for their own uses. Calling on the name of God in prayer,

124

for instance, can mean attempting to make God a tool for our purposes'.[13]

As I gaze upon the throne of God, I say nothing. I do not attempt to call out to God or to address him by name. To name God would be to have an element of control in the situation. The namelessness of God shows me that it is God who is in control.

The one who sits there has the appearance of jasper and carnelian

I love the exotic colours emanating from the throne of God. Jasper is an opaque quartz, a precious stone. Carnelian is a translucent red stone. Jasper and carnelian are the prismatic colours through which the unapproachable light of God's glory is reflected (1 Timothy 6.16).

As I worship at God's footstool, I know that God sees me in the best possible light. 'Lives that have been defaced by sin into blurred charcoal outlines are now seen in their true colours. Every faded tint and wavering line is restored to original sharpness and hue.'[14] I bathe in the healing light of God's acceptance.

A rainbow, resembling an emerald, encircles the throne

I spend a moment to look above the throne, where a velvety-green rainbow glows like a huge halo. I worship God in the silence because the rainbow is a sign of God's mercy. I recall God's words in Genesis 9.12–16, and hear them as personally addressing me:

> 'This is the sign of the covenant I am making between me and you and every living creature with you, a covenant for all generations to come: I have set my rainbow in the clouds, and it will be the sign of the covenant between me and the earth. Whenever I bring clouds over the earth and the rainbow appears in the clouds, I will remember my covenant between me and you and all living creatures of every kind. Never again will the waters become a flood to destroy all life. Whenever the rainbow appears in the clouds, I will see it and remember the everlasting covenant between God and all living creatures of every kind on the earth.'

The emerald rainbow encircling God's throne is a reminder that God accepts me because of his mercy revealed in Christ Jesus. Jesus has drunk from the cup of God's wrath. Therefore I know the truth of Hebrews 4.16: 'Let us approach the throne of grace with confidence, so that we may receive mercy and find grace to help us in our time of need' (4.16). How I thank God that his throne is a place of grace not of judgement!

Surrounding the throne are twenty-four other thrones

As my eyes shift from what I can see above the throne, I begin to notice that there are twenty-four other thrones stationed around the main, royal throne. On these thrones sit twenty-four elders. Twelve of them are the representatives of the old covenant. They are presumably the original leaders of the twelve tribes of Israel. The other twelve are the representatives of the new covenant. They are obviously the twelve apostles. These elders are dressed in white with crowns of gold upon their heads.

As I look at these elders, I remember the first line of a hymn, 'O welcome all ye noble saints of old'.

From the throne come flashes of lightning, rumblings and peals of thunder

From seeing I turn to hearing. The lightning and thunder are deafening. I am only feet away from the throne from which they are exploding. I have to put my hands over my ears. I sense the awesome power of God as the lightning spears its way from the throne across the vast expanse of heaven. I sense the greatness of God as I hear the thunder crash around me. I have a sense of my vulnerability, my mortality and my finitude.

Before the throne seven lamps are blazing . . . and there is what looks like a sea of glass, clear as crystal

But then something strange. After the tremendous movement and energy of the thunder and the lightning comes the still calm of the heavenly counterparts of the *menorah* and the brazen sea. I gaze upon the burning flames in the seven golden candlesticks and ask the Spirit to minister revelation. I stand before the crystal sea and ask the Spirit to minister rest. I breathe in the air of heaven, and listen to the quietest hint of wave upon shore. In a moment of heavenly stasis, I rest in the presence of the King of Kings.

Before the throne are four living creatures

Suddenly I see them. Four strange creatures around the centre of God's throne. The first of these is like a lion, the second is like an ox, the third is like a man, the fourth is like a flying eagle. They are covered with eyes and are all able to fly. Indeed, they are actually flying just above the throne of God, and above the twenty-four thrones surrounding God's throne.

I see four groups of beings around the throne. First of all the four living creatures. Then the twenty-four elders. Then the 'many angels, numbering thousands upon thousands, and ten thousand times ten thousand' (Revelation 5.11). Finally, 'every creature in heaven and on earth and under the earth and on the sea'.

I see these as ever-increasing circles of praise. At the very centre of this praise is God upon his throne. Then there are the four living creatures directly around and above the throne. After that are the twenty-four elders. Following them are the myriads of angels. Following them is the whole of creation.

The four living creatures are, in a strange sense, a comfort to me. As Eugene Petersen puts it:

> The act of worship gathers into its centring rituals and harmonizing rhythms every aspect of creation. Worship does not divide the spiritual from the natural, it coordinates them. Nature and supernature, creation and covenant, elders and animals are all gathered. Worship that scorns creation is impoverished. The rabble of creation 'red in tooth and claw' comes to order before the throne and finds itself more itself: each creature is alert (full of eyes) and soaring (six wings). In George Herbert's words: 'All creatures of my God and King, lift up your voice and sing!'[15]

Day and night, they never stop saying, 'Holy, holy, holy!'
The noise of the thunder fades and a new sound is heard – the
sound of the four living creatures worshipping God. Now I begin
to notice the variety of worship around God's throne. The four
living creatures and the twenty-four elders declare rather than sing
their praises. Their declarations are united statements of adoration
of God the Holy One. The four living creatures start this worship
with the words, 'Holy, holy, holy is the Lord Almighty, who was,
and is, and is to come'. As soon as the twenty-four elders hear this,
they fall down and proclaim,

> You are worthy, our Lord and God,
> to receive glory and honour and power,
> for you created all things,
> and by your will they were created
> and have their being.

This is worship which is said not sung. It is worship addressed to
God the Creator.

The next three outbursts of worship are different. They are all in
the form of song, and they follow directly after the appearance
of the Lamb of God in Revelation 5.1–7. When the four living
creatures and the twenty-four elders understand that Jesus, the
Lamb of God, is the only one in heaven and on earth worthy
enough to receive the scroll, they join forces to sing a spontaneous,
new song:

> You are worthy to take the scroll
> and to open its seals,
> because you were slain,
> and with your blood you purchased
> men for God
> from every tribe and language and
> people and nation.
> You have made them to be a kingdom

and priests to serve our God,
and they will reign on the earth.

As soon as the angels hear this song, they in turn sing their own song in a loud voice:

Worthy is the Lamb, who was slain,
to receive power and wealth
and wisdom and strength
and honour and glory and praise!

These two songs in Revelation 5 are addressed to Jesus, the Lamb of God. If the worship of the first two songs address God the Creator, the second two address God the Redeemer. In the last song, however, both the God who reigns on the throne, and the Lamb who is at the centre of the throne, are honoured in one and the same song. Now it is the turn of the whole of creation to sing a final, great doxology:

To him who sits on the throne and to
    the Lamb
be praise and honour and glory and power,
for ever and ever!

In all of this, I cannot help noticing that the worship of the creatures, the elders and the angels is about Calvary. I see Jesus, 'a Lamb, looking as if it had been slain, standing in the centre of the throne, encircled by the four living creatures and the elders'. When the Lamb of God appears, the four living creatures and the twenty-four elders worship him for having purchased people for God from every tribe and language and people and nation. They shout 'Worthy is the Lamb who was slain'. Calvary is therefore the central cause of sung worship in heaven. Indeed, heaven is not allowed to forget the wounds of Jesus.

Crown him the Lord of love;
Behold his hands and side,

Those wounds yet visible above
In beauty glorified:
No angel in the sky
Can fully bear that sight,
But downward bends his burning eye
At mysteries so bright.

From Meditation to Contemplation

Of all the forms of prayer in this book, beholding the throne of God can seem the most daunting of all. It is hard not to feel threatened by it. Surely this kind of prayer is literally light years away from all but the most spiritual.

In practice, this discipline does require work. We start with the Scriptures open before us and we go through Revelation 4 verse by verse, allowing the passage to go deep inside us. Gradually, over the course of weeks, the passage becomes so familiar to us that we no longer need our Bibles in front of us. Instead we work our way through the vision with the help of both our memory and our imagination. Once we have got this far, we have made the transition from meditation to contemplation. Meditation is a fixed attention on a passage in the Bible or on some aspect of creation and being. Contemplation is a devotional awareness of God which is not tied to a biblical text or a visible object. Contemplation is pure, unaided adoration.

After weeks of reading we therefore start to practise anointed recollection. Once we have come this far, the adventure begins. Many people at this stage begin to find that beholding the throne is something which they look forward to immensely. One friend of mine who heard me speak on this subject told me that it is this form of prayer which he enjoys most. It has proved an invaluable source of personal refreshment and renewal for him. Every time is different. When he is feeling in need of encouragement, he stops and contemplates the emerald rainbow, and reminds himself of God's love. At other times when he is feeling frail, he pauses at the throne, imagining the thunder and lightning, and remembers God's power. Sometimes when he is feeling tired and overworked, he pictures the sea of glass, and drinks in the stillness where God is.

In teaching this discipline to his church, this friend told me that he likens it to shopping. When we go shopping, we walk through the streets and the arcades and stop at those shops which catch our attention. We do not attempt to go into every shop which we pass and browse there. The same is true for beholding the throne in prayer. Once we have become familiar with the passage, the point is not to try and spend a lot of time focusing on each aspect of the vision. Rather, we should allow the Spirit to show us which part of this Scripture will most nourish us today.

I find this a helpful analogy. It makes our priestly ministry in the holy of holies a more accessible and a less daunting one.

From Contemplation to Vision

Beholding the Lord in prayer therefore requires work and discipline. After a while, meditation turns to contemplation. If we are really blessed, there may come a time when contemplation turns to vision.

What happens when we move on from a contemplative and anointed remembrance of Revelation 4 to an actual vision of heaven? Here we move from the symbols themselves to the realities to which they point. We move from the signifiers to their signified. It is a very rare privilege, and not everyone will experience it this side of eternity. But just occasionally, God will lead someone who regularly practises this discipline into the highest form of divine union which a human being can attain: a vision of some aspect of the heavenly realm.

Recently, a member of my church was receiving prayer ministry. She had heard my teaching on beholding the throne and had started to develop the practice of 'dreaming of heaven'. As she was being prayed for she saw the following:

> It came to me early in the ministry prayers. My eyes were closed, and ten feet in front of me appeared a large lion, walking from left to right. His face didn't leave mine. He kept looking at me as

he proudly, triumphantly, powerfully and majestically walked to and fro. I was overwhelmed by a sense of his royal dignity. I felt safe and relaxed. This was Jesus, Immanuel, God with us.

The next thing I noticed were three winged animals about ten feet above him, in the two o'clock position (at the time, I saw them as seraphs). I noticed the wings more than anything. I couldn't see their bodies except to say that they were rounded at the edges. They only moved very slightly. They appeared weightless. The lion was a glorious golden colour with a wonderfully long mane.

Apart from the lion and the three strange animals, the rest seemed to be dark, especially the background.

Next, I heard a distant trumpet sound. I couldn't pick out any notes (it was a major key, however). Somehow I felt that there were three instruments playing. The music seemed to be saying, 'Praise him! Praise him!' It all felt regal, but welcoming too!

This vision of Jesus is extremely important to me and I'll never forget it. I still see a vision of the lion occasionally when in prayer.

This woman had moved from meditation to contemplation, and from contemplation to vision. Having filled her mind with heavenly realities, she was ready to be anointed with a vision of the Lion of Judah before the throne. Maybe you and I will one day have this privilege too.

The Door to Eternity

So why is it important to have a go at beholding the throne of God in prayer?

One of the greatest reasons for attempting this form of prayer is the simple fact that it gives us a glimpse of our eternal destiny. A daily ministry of 'dreaming of heaven' is not a form of escapism in which we become so heavenly-minded that we are no earthly use, as the saying goes. It is a way of facing the reality of our mortality. As King David put it,

You have made my days a mere handbreath;
the span of my years is as nothing before you.
Each man's life is but a breath (Psalm 39.5).

Beholding the Lord is not only a means of helping us to confront our finitude, it is also a way of preparing us for heaven. I find in my ministry that there are few people today who know what the Bible says about heaven. Is it any surprise, then, that our society is so hope-less and pessimistic? If the Church cannot be certain about the nature of its ultimate future, then who can?

The virtue of a daily focus on the throne of God is that it constantly reminds us of what will happen to us after God has raised us from the sleep of death on the last day. From that day onwards, we will be worshipping with that great cloud of witnesses gathered in circles of praise around God's throne. This means that every time we enter the most holy place to behold the Lord we are making ready for our eternal home, where we will see endless theophanies which will feel more real than reality.

New Heaven, New Earth

Nothing has reminded me more powerfully of this need to fix our hearts on eternity than the recent death of the daughter of a Christian friend. Not long ago, I got a 'phone call. My friend Duncan just uttered the words, 'Ericka's dead'. I put down the 'phone immediately and hurried around to his house. When I arrived there, Ericka was lying dead in her mother's arms. She was only twelve years' old.

Duncan and I sat on the bed for a long time in silence. Ericka looked peaceful after her long struggle with disease. Even so, all we could do was weep quietly. But then something very powerful happened. Helen, Ericka's mother, held her daughter close and shut her eyes. As she did so, beautiful words of hope started to flow from her mouth:

'Then I saw a new heaven and a new earth, for the first heaven and the first earth had passed away, and there was no longer any sea. I saw the Holy City, the new Jerusalem, coming down out of heaven from God, prepared as a bride beautifully dressed for her husband. And I heard a loud voice from the throne saying, 'Now the dwelling of God is with men, and he will live with them. They will be his people and God himself will be with them and be their God. He will wipe every tear from their eyes. There will be no more death or mourning or crying or pain, for the old order of things has passed away.'

These words from Revelation 21 changed the whole atmosphere of the bedroom. Although they did not remove the sense of loss, they opened up a horizon of hope where before there was only dereliction. They helped us to stand with Ericka, just for a moment, on the threshold of a great eternity.

The Gate of Heaven

I do urge you, then, to spend time in the most holy place, contemplating the throne of God, preparing for heaven. Whenever you behold the Lord in prayer, you enter an atmosphere of worship which is not wholly of this world. You enter an atmosphere which is thick with angels. That is why it is important to spend time entering the door to eternity in prayer. Every time you go through this initial entry-point, whether it is indoors or out on the hills, you will be able to say with Jacob, 'How awesome is this place! This is none other than the house of God, and this is the gate of heaven' (Genesis 28.17).

CONCLUSION

God said to the people of Israel, 'You will be for me a kingdom of priests and a holy nation' (Exodus 19.6). This book has been an attempt to give both a theological and a practical framework for living out our royal priesthood in daily prayer.

In the first two chapters, I showed how prayer must begin: with invoking the Spirit, thanking the Father, and praising Christ's name. It is interesting to note that when King David appointed priests to minister before the ark of the covenant, he gave them precisely this task: 'To invoke, to thank, and to praise the Lord, the God of Israel' (2 Chronicles 16.4). This exactly corresponds to the initial stages of our priestly ministry. We first of all invoke the Holy Spirit in the words of the *epiklesis*, 'Come, Holy Spirit'. We do this so that our prayers may be spontaneous as well as structured.

We secondly offer up our *berakhot* or prayers of thanksgiving. As we recollect the previous day, we give thanks that out of the fullness of his grace, God has given us one blessing after another: spiritual, physical, emotional, material, intellectual, and relational blessings. As we do so, we enter through the gates of God's holy presence and prepare to offer up a sacrifice of praise.

Thirdly, we lift our eyes away from what God has done to focus upon who he is. We start to praise him for his name. We pray the prayer of high Christology as we exalt the Lord Jesus Christ using the titles and names ascribed to him in Scripture. Some days this praise is a prayer of the mind, rooted in theological reflection; on other days it may well be the prayer of the heart, a childlike 'I love you, Father'. At other times it may be the prayer of the Spirit, the adorational use of tongues. Sometimes it will be all three. Whatever the case, it will be a ministry of praise in the court of the priests.

After these three ministries of invoking, thanking and praising, we turn to the ministry of confession. We come before the altar of sacrifice, the Cross on which the Prince of Glory died. We make a vow with ourselves that we will be honest before the Lord. We remember that 'confession without change is just a game'. We scrutinize our lives in the light of God's Word and his Spirit. We make our confession to God, firmly resolved – with his help – to put our sins to death. We then receive his pardon and his cleansing, as we wash in the bronze laver of water.

Now we are ready to walk with Jesus, our Great High Priest, into the sanctuary building. We stop at the golden table of shew-bread and petition for our own physical, material and emotional needs. We proceed to the golden lampstands where we pray for the Father to meet our spiritual needs. We pray for the good gifts of the Spirit, for more of the Spirit's fruit, and for greater intimacy in the vine of Jesus Christ. Then we walk to the focal point of the holy place, the golden altar of incense which stands before the veil to the innermost sanctuary. Here we offer up our intercessions for the Church, the community, the city, the country, the continents and for creation.

At last we kneel before the entrance to the most holy place. The veil is open as we prepare to enter. Christ's atoning sacrifice has given us freedom of access. So now we proceed into the innermost sanctuary, walking with reverence and holy fear. We call to mind the vision of the throne of God in Revelation 4, and spend time allowing the Spirit to open our eyes to the heavenly realm. Some-times this will be a matter of biblical meditation; at other times it will be a matter of unaided contemplation. Just occasionally we will actually see visions and dream dreams. We should be open to whatever the God of Surprises may do in us.

Preparing to Minister in the World

Once we have finished our ministry in the Temple, there is only one more thing to do. We will need to rest for a few minutes before we attempt to go on to anything else. Priestly prayer requires work and discipline. It involves expending our physical, emotional and spiritual energy. Before we move on to other things, it is therefore vital that we spend time in rest and listening.

There is a beautiful picture of this kind of restful prayer in John 13, John's narrative of the Last Supper. During the business of the meal, we catch a glimpse of the beloved disciple leaning 'on the bosom of Jesus'. He is the only one who can hear the quiet words of the Saviour because he is the only one who is lying in his presence. Peter cannot hear Jesus. He has to ask the beloved disciple what Jesus has been saying.

This cameo of the intimacy contains tremendous significance in a very few words. It teaches us that those who lie close to the heart of Jesus will be in tune with his heart; those who rest in his presence will receive his revelation. For this reason, it is helpful to finish prayer with a time of resting, of drinking in the stillness, of listening to the promptings of the Spirit. In the quietness of the aftermath of all these priestly ministries, we can lay the coming day before the Lord and listen out for the guidance and the wisdom which he may, in his mercy, provide. As we do this, we become one of Christ's beloved disciples, one of his 'bosom pals'.[1] We hear what the Father is saying concerning how we can best commend the Gospel in this post-Christian world. We prepare to be sent out into the world, to work as priests of the kingdom.

Representing God to the World

This last point about our ministry to the world is important. Leslie Newbiggin has reminded us that 'The office of a priest is to stand before God on behalf of people and to stand before people on behalf of God'.[2] In other words, priesthood is not only about bringing people to God in prayer (the substance of this book). It is also about bringing something of the reign of God to where people are.

Thus our priesthood is not confined to the sacred parts of life; it is also to be exercised in what is called the secular realm. As Newbiggin goes on to say, 'the exercise of this priesthood is not within the walls of the church but the daily business of the world. It is only in this way that the public life of the world, its accepted habits and assumptions, can be challenged by the gospel and brought under the searching light of the truth as it has been revealed in Jesus'.[3] In the final analysis, 'it is the whole Church which is called to be – in Christ – a royal priesthood . . . every member of the body is called to the exercise of this priesthood, and . . . this priesthood is to be exercised in the daily life and work of Christians and in the secular business of the world'.[4]

I agree with these sentiments entirely. Priesthood is not only about ministering *to* God in the sanctuary. It is also about ministering *for* God in the desert. That is why Paul speaks of the 'priestly duty of proclaiming the Gospel of God, so that the Gentiles might become an offering acceptable to God, sanctified by the Holy Spirit' (Romans 15.16). The words 'priestly duty' (*leiturgos*, from which we get 'liturgy') should strike a chord within us. This book has been a detailed description about priestly duties, duties which involve representing people before God. But here Paul talks about priestly duties in the context of representing God to people, in the context of preaching the Gospel to the Gentiles.

Jimmy Dunn has pointed out that there is an intense concentration of cultic, Temple terminology in these verses: 'priestly duty', 'an offering acceptable to God', 'sanctified by the Holy Spirit'. By applying this language to the ministry of evangelism, Paul confirms that for him 'the cultic barrier between sacred and secular has been broken through and left behind. And by speaking of the Gentiles as themselves the altar of sacrifice in the Temple . . . Paul confirms that for him the culturally defined barrier between peoples, between Jew and Gentile, had been broken through and left behind'.[5] For Paul, sharing the Gospel is the work of a priest (*hierourgeo*).

In the final analysis, the example of St Paul is a strong argument against erecting an iron curtain between the sacred and the secular. Our priesthood is not to be a secret and sectarian ministry. It is to be a bold and open ministry of service in the world.

So after all is said and done, we need to pray:

> Send us out
> in the power of your Spirit,

to live and work
to your praise and glory. Amen.

APPENDIX

Using the Temple Model in Corporate Worship

This book has really been designed for enriching one's *personal* prayer life through the use of Temple symbolism. However, this Temple model can also be utilized in acts of public worship. What follows is a breakdown of the event.

Preparation

I have always had access to an overhead projector when I have used the design of the Temple in public worship. This is essential because all the illustrations in this book have been laser copied and then photocopied on to OHP acetates. These visuals help people to see the act of worship as a gradual journey into the holy of holies.

Having prepared the OHP, screen and acetates, the next thing to do is to create a worshipful ambience through the use of black-outs and candles. Blacking-out windows is important. The light from the OHP and candles creates a sense of holy awe even as people come into the church or the meeting-room. No other lighting is usually necessary. Particularly useful is a focal point. We use the altar, placing a large number of night-lights around the foot of the altar cross. Quiet music is appropriate as people come in, either from a small worship group or from a tape recorder. Flute and keyboard is a particularly powerful combination.

Worship

Once people are settled and the music has stopped playing, the first stage is a matter of waiting on the Spirit. Some kind of invocation can be used, either in words or in song (e.g. 'Spirit of the Living God', 'More Love, More Power', or 'Veni Sancte Spiritus'). Alternatively, silence can be golden.

From this point on the worship progresses smoothly until the end of the confession. A period of thoughtful thanksgiving and praise can be run together very effectively, using both ancient and modern hymns, and open declarations of worship from the floor. Spontaneity (being led by the Spirit) is very important at this point, as indeed it is all the way through. Encouraging people to reflect on God's blessings is the place to start; then you can move on to God's nature.

In the confession, liturgy is important. Silent reflection on where we stand with God is followed by a set prayer, either from a liturgical service or from the Scriptures (e.g. Psalm 51). At this point some teaching from Scripture is necessary. Teaching from the Scriptures and from the saints about prayer is particularly effective in this setting. Teaching on one of the spiritual disciplines involved in the Temple model is also helpful (thanksgiving, praise, confession, petition, intercession, devotion).

Usually, in St Mark's parish where I work, we use the church building itself. At this stage in the service, everyone moves from the nave up to the choir stalls in front of the candle-lit altar. People either sit in the stalls or on cushions on the floor. There is always a great sense of family as we squeeze together into the area in front of the sanctuary. There are no hymn books or OHPs here. We are on our own in the holy place. We have each other and we have the Lord.

There then follows a period of silence for about twenty minutes. In this silence, people are encouraged to listen to the promptings of the Spirit and to speak them out. Usually a common theme emerges in the pictures and words that are shared. This theme is then picked up by the inter-cessor, who encourages us to intercede in response to the words. That way the congregation learns to discern the mind of Christ, to enter into that divine stream of consciousness which I wrote about in Chapter 4. Intercession is better made aloud, though those who want to think, sigh or pray inaudibly in tongues are encouraged.

When the intercessions come to an end, the leader conducts a medi-tation on the throne of God in Revelation 4. This is best done as a voice-over: in other words, one musician installs a keyboard in the sanctuary and plays a melody quietly under the voice of the worship leader. The melody should be one that can feed into a song like 'Holy, Holy, Holy' which focuses on the throne of God in heaven. This climactic part of the service is best conducted with everyone standing, hands raised (if comfortable with that) to heaven.

After the meditation there is silence and resting in the presence of the Lord. The Grace then follows, with all joining hands and looking at each other.

Finally, the same music that was played at the beginning of the service is played again, as a signal that the worship event is now over.

Response

After the worship, it is vital to elicit responses from the people who participated. Some words do not get shared because of shyness, or a leader's lack of sensitivity. Sometimes there are helpful comments to make concerning the development of a more creative and workable way of doing things. Feedback, in other words, is crucial.

NOTES

Introduction

1 Saint Teresa of Avila, *The Interior Castle*, trans. by John Vernard (Sydney, 1988), pp. 26–7.
2 Ibid., p. 1.

1 The Gates of Thanksgiving

1 Quoted in *1500 Illustrations for Preaching and Teaching*, compiled by Robert Blackhouse (London: Marshall Pickering, 1991), p. 294.
2 R. Lovelace, *Dynamics of Spiritual Life* (Exeter: Paternoster Press, 1979), p. 155.
3 Ibid., p. 155.
4 A. Murray, *The Prayer Life* (London: Marshall, Morgan & Scott, 1968), p. 53.
5 T.S. Eliot, *The Use of Poetry and the Use of Criticism* (London: Faber, 1975), p. 146.
6 See C. Di Sante, *Jewish Prayer* (New York: Paulist Press, 1985), p. viii.
7 Ibid., p. 104.
8 A. Murray, ibid., p. 54.
9 C. Di Sante, ibid., p. 38.
10 S.T. Coleridge (13 July 1834, twelve days before his death). Cited in L. Weatherhead, *A Private House of Prayer* (London: Hodder & Stoughton, 1966), p. 217.
11 C. Di Sante, ibid., p. 139.

2 The Court of Praise

1 Saint Teresa of Avila, *The Interior Castle*, p. 7.
2 M. Borg, *Jesus. A New Vision* (San Francisco: Harper & Row, 1987), p. 1.

3 D. Icke, *Truth Vibrations* (London: Aquarian Press, 1991), pp. 115–16.

4 See, for example, T.C. Horton and C.E. Hulbert, *The Wonderful Names of our Wonderful Lord* (Los Angeles: Grant Publishing House, 1925), P.W. Krumwiede, *Names of Jesus* (Philadelphia: United Lutheran Publishing House, 1927), J. Large, *Two Hundred and Eighty Titles and Symbols of Christ* (Grand Rapids: Baker Book House, 1959), C.J. Rolls, *Time's Noblest Name* (New Jersey: Loizeaux Brothers, 1965) and, most recently, E.L. Towns, *The Name of Jesus* (Denver: Accent Publications, 1987).

5 K. Barth, *Evangelical Theology* (Edinburgh: T. & T. Clark, 1979), pp. 161–70.

6 For more on 'the prayer of the heart', see R. Foster, *Prayer* (London: Hodder & Stoughton 1992), p. 137.

3 The Altar of Sacrifice

1 L.T. Johnson, *Sharing Possessions* (London: SCM Press, 1986), p. 49.

2 R. Foster, *Money, Sex, Power* (London: Hodder & Stoughton, 1985).

3 C. Di Sante, *Jewish Prayer*, op. cit., p. 216.

4 The Holy Place

1 I am indebted for this insight to J. Rea, *The Holy Spirit in the Bible* (London: Marshall Pickering, 1990), pp. 86–7.

2 Cited in *1500 Illustrations for Preaching and Teaching*, compiled by Robert Backhouse, op. cit., p. 295.

5 The Holy of Holies

1 M. Barker, *The Gate of Heaven* (London: SPCK, 1991), p. 154.

2 M. Barker, ibid., pp. 155–7.

3 There is a long history behind the practice of beholding the Lord in prayer. Open any copy of Julian of Norwich's *Revelations of Divine Love* and you will see how important beholding Christ was to her. Beholding prayer is therefore a common theme in the mystical tradition. Recently, however, it has surfaced again in a charismatic context, notably in Mike Bickle's teaching on the throne of God.

Mike Bickle is senior pastor of the Kansas City Fellowship. However, I sense that many people have developed their own discipline of beholding quite independently of these traditions. After speaking on 'beholding the throne' at a leader's day in Sheffield, a clergyman wrote the following letter to me:

> Since becoming a Christian I have always been encouraged to develop a discipline of Bible reading and prayer. This has normally taken the form of a 'quiet time' with notes of some form to organize my reading, and help my walk with the Lord.
>
> However, I became increasingly dissatisfied with my 'quiet time' and found that it was becoming more of a study. This was especially so since I was spending more time in study preparation for leading Bible studies and preaching. I felt that the quiet time was becoming a 'thinking' time, full of the noise of my thoughts and wise words from those who prepared the notes.
>
> While at theological college, I was challenged to explore silence and meditation, which led me into a new experience of that special time set aside to be with God.
>
> In these times of silence I increasingly used visual aids to help me into the silence – things like pictures, pieces of wood, candles, etc. These seemed to my artistic nature to open up areas within myself that had so far remained unreleased.
>
> At the same time, my doctrine lecturer greatly challenged my view of the Holy Trinity and asked me if I could paint a picture that depicted the Trinity.
>
> The idea of something visual greatly excited me and so I chose the theme of 'Praying in the Trinity'. At that time I had found myself praying with perhaps one of the persons of the Trinity in the front of my mind, most typically 'my Saviour Jesus Christ'. I was looking for a way of increasing my awareness of the unity of the Trinity.
>
> As I read through the Book of Revelation, many images flew out at me, while also being struck by the thinking that lay behind the work of Rublev, the Russian icon painter.
>
> It was at that time that I painted my own icon.
>
> I still use the 'icon' I created in order to remind myself that, as I come to God, I come before the throne from which flows 'the river of the water of life' (Rev. 21.1). I stand in that river, conscious of the Lamb of God on one side and the Holy Spirit with

wings of fire on the other. The three thrones stand on a circle, a mark of their oneness. The Father's throne contains no image but from it is the source of all light (Rev. 21.5).

4   J. McKay, *When the Veil is Taken Away* (unpublished booklet), p. 33.
5   R. Lovelace, *Dynamics of the Spiritual Life*, op. cit., pp. 85–6.
6   In S. Parenti (ed.), *Praying with the Orthodox Tradition* (London: SPCK, 1989), p. xi.
7   Ibid., p. 5.
8   C.S. Lewis, *The Lion, the Witch and the Wardrobe* (London: Collins, 1981 edition), p. 77.
9   Cited in R. Foster, *Prayer*, op. cit., p. 166.
10 G. Ladd, *The Presence of the Future* (Grand Rapids: Eerdmans, 1974).
11 P. Tillich, *The Eternal Now* (London: SCM Press, 1963), p. 81.
12 Ibid., p. 83.
13 Ibid., p. 77.
14 E. Petersen, *Reversed Thunder* (San Francisco: Harper & Row, 1988), p. 62.
15 Ibid., p. 62.

Conclusion

1   J.A.T. Robinson refers to the beloved disciple as Jesus' 'bosom friend' in *The Priority of John* (London: SCM Press, 1985), p. 119; this is on the basis that the disciple rests on the bosom of Jesus and is singled out as 'beloved'.
2   L. Newbiggin, *The Gospel in a Pluralist Society* (London: SPCK, 1992), p. 230.
3   Ibid., p. 230.
4   Ibid., p. 235.
5   J. Dunn, *Romans 9–16*, Word Biblical Commentary (38B) (Dallas: Word Books, 1988), p. 867.